CLEM SUNTER

# THE NEW CENTURY

*Quest for the High Road*

HUMAN & ROUSSEAU
TAFELBERG

First published in 1992 jointly by
Human & Rousseau (Pty) Ltd, State House, 3-9 Rose Street, Cape Town
and Tafelberg Publishers Ltd, 28 Wale Street, Cape Town

Cover photograph of the author courtesy of PA Gallo & Company
Colour diagrams generated on DTP by The Desktop Studio, Sea Point
Set on DTP in 10.5 on 13 pt Plantin
and positives supplied by Diatype Setting, Cape Town
Printed and bound by National Book Printers, Goodwood, Cape
First edition, first impression 1992

ISBN 0 7981 3005 9

TO MY FAMILY

AND

JOHN YOUNG
*(so many songs
we forgot to play)*

# Contents

# Acknowledgements

This book is a tribute to all the remarkable people who over the years have contributed to Anglo American Corporation's scenario programme.

To Pierre Wack and Ted Newland who introduced scenario planning to us at the end of 1982.

To Edouard Parker who shared with us his unique approach to political risk analysis.

To Hughes de Jouvenal, Michael Kaser, Henry Ergas, Heinrich Vogel, Alain de Vulpain, Michael Hinks-Edwards and PA Technology for their expertise on specific topics relating to our global studies.

To Allan Newey, Luc Smets, Paul Missen, Ian Emsley, Yugo Kovach, Steve Landsberg, Frank Meakin, Jackie Steinitz, Gil Devlin and other members of Anglo's Research and Economic Services Department in London for consistently excellent research on world affairs.

To Bruce Scott and Peter Schwartz for their friendly encouragement over the years.

To Michael O'Dowd and Bobby Godsell who adapted Edouard Parker's methodology to create the classic "High Road" and "Low Road" scenarios for South Africa.

To Michael Spicer and Jim Buys for assistance in spreading the "High Road" message and, with Margie Keeton, Gavin Keeton, Don Ncube and Colin Beeforth, for their work in updating the scenarios.

To Brian Huntley, Roy Siegfried, Rick Lomba, Jock Danckwerts, Dave Dewar, George Ellis, Symond Fiske, Tim Hart, Fred Kruger, Mike Mentis, Elize Moody, Graham Noble, John Raimondo, Roland Schulze, Butch Smuts, Rob Soutter and Jenny Thomson for their invaluable contributions on the environment.

To Michael O'Connor and Grace Sutherland for co-ordinating the entire project.

To Koos Human, Danie van Niekerk, Hans Büttner and Jürgen

Fomm who've made the writing of the three books on scenarios an absolute pleasure.

To Peter Gallo and Marie Bruyns – who've done likewise in respect of the production of the three videos.

To Pam Herr who achieved her ambition of filling the Nico Malan Opera House in Cape Town to capacity for one of my "High Road" presentations and to all the other organisers of my talks over the years.

To Pat Meneghini for typing this manuscript and Drusilla Wildgoose for her assistance in producing the graphics for the many in-house scenario presentations.

To Anglo American Corporation for never wavering in its moral and financial support for the project, and for generously giving me total discretion over the material. In that sense, the views expressed in this book are the team's and my own – they do not reflect a "corporate viewpoint".

And finally, to the countless men and women who carry the torch for the "High Road".

Will the New Century be greeted by a "golden dawn" or an "endless night"?

Now is the time to ask.

# Introduction

I've been head of scenario planning at Anglo American Corporation for nine years now. It seems a lot of water has flowed under the bridge since I first met the two gurus of scenario planning, Pierre Wack and Ted Newland, who introduced us to the process at Anglo. The Berlin wall has been demolished, Germany has been reunited, the Cold War is over for the time being, Mexico's star is rising and South Africa is in transition. Most assuredly, the future is not what it used to be.

Our scenario team now acts as the company's radar system, scanning the future business environment for possible surprises and pitfalls and generally sensitising our employees to change. Change is an inherent part of business, but every company has a certain resistance to it. It's a natural human condition. Scenario planning is there to lower that resistance by stretching the imagination. It is therefore a very useful process since change in any form – economic, political or technological – can be an ally or a foe. Change can promote a company's fortunes if identified in advance and handled intelligently; or it can bankrupt a company.

## The Purpose of Scenario Planning

The purpose of scenario planning is to use language to change attitudes to change decisions to change the course of events for the better. If this chain is broken in any way, the process is rendered worthless. For example, suppose a scenario-ist projects a scenario of an avoidable catastrophe, which on the one hand is so dull that nobody listens to it but on the other hand is quite correct so that the company is devastated; the scenario-ist should have saved his energy. Scenarios must have a fair chance of shifting the mindset (or paradigm to use scenario parlance) of the teams that make up a business organisation. The message to be conveyed is: your life will be directly

1

## PURPOSE OF SCENARIO PLANNING

➡ **Stories about the future**
➡ **Influence attitudes**
➡ **Change decisions**
➡ **Improve actual course of events**

*Chart 1*

affected by the decisions you make – now. But before you make those decisions, be open to new ideas; for the future may not be as you imagine.

The world is changed not by people who are right but by people who can convince others that they are right. That is why language is as important as content. The scenario titles must be catchy enough to establish a common idiom and the phrases punchy enough to strike a chord of urgency. Each individual watching a scenario presentation should see the challenge and opportunity ahead and realise that he or she can play an essential part in the changing world – however small. The job is done if that individual is inspired to go out and use his or her own talents to add to the bigger picture.

Scenario planning is quite different from strategic planning. Scenarios are shortish poems of possible futures to sway the listener to be flexible in outlook; strategic plans are intricate essays of steps to be taken to achieve certain goals. The two functions require people with very different skills. An ideal scenario planner is an iconoclast, dedicated to uprooting complacency which spreads like a weed with success, killing companies and nations that thought they would be on top forever. A wise man once gave me the following piece of advice: "When approaching a sacred cow, examine it closely for you have three options. You can milk it if it is still useful, put it out to pasture if it is harmless, or send it to the abattoir if it's a liability. But never take a sacred cow for granted!"

### Multiple Pasts, Multiple Futures

We all know that in actual fact there is one past and one future. That does not stop historians arguing about what the actual past was; nor does it deter each of us from spinning several possibilities for the future. In the "world of perception" we look back on multiple pasts, and forward to multiple futures.

A story I was told recently by a retired headmaster about one of his experiences at high school makes the point beautifully. He had just started an English lesson in which he was teaching the class about the pressure on journalists to record events correctly. His dissertation was interrupted by one of the school's known troublemakers walking in to fetch schoolbooks he'd left after a previous class. The headmaster was extremely annoyed and remonstrated with the boy for being so rude, at which the boy reacted by telling the headmaster in no uncertain terms that his books mattered more to him than the lesson underway. At this point he walked out, followed by the headmaster, and there were sounds of a scuffle in the passage outside. The headmaster re-entered the room with a bleeding nose and immediately asked the class to do an exercise in real journalism. He said he wanted the events precisely recorded so that when he took action he had the testimony of plenty of witnesses. Needless to say, the class complied with alacrity, meanwhile dreaming up what terrible fate awaited the mischief-maker. It was only after they had all handed in their versions of the events that the headmaster told them the whole exercise had been set up beforehand and the blood was tomato sauce. But the interesting result was that in 20 of the 28 essays the writer had actually seen the mischief-maker belt the headmaster on the nose!

This example highlights the tendency in all of us to perceive facts poorly, particularly if we're emotionally involved in a situation. Scenario planning, by providing a forum for raising seemingly peripheral issues which end up being central to the debate, helps to sharpen our judgment about the past and what may flow from it in the future. In the example just given, the issue was clearly whether any of the pupils had actually seen the headmaster being hit. In a discussion of possible scenarios of how the miscreant would be punished, perhaps the fact that no one had seen the punch being delivered would have surfaced. In this case the pupils might have recognised that they were victims of a conspiracy without having to be informed of it. Scenarios, like parables, provide deep insights.

It is quite a thought that of the top 100 companies in the United States in 1956 only 29 are still in the top 100 in 1992. Of the top 100 companies outside the US in 1957 only 27 were still there in 1989. Joseph Schumpeter called it the "creative destruction" of capitalism. Thus, 71 American and 73 non-American companies, despite their enormous financial resources and reservoir of human skills 35 years ago, were subsequently lapped in the economic race. Perhaps there was no way that some of them could keep up: like ageing athletes they had to drop by the wayside. But in many cases, myopic vision and inflexible strategic thinking precipitated the fall. In fact I'm sure none of the managements of those companies in 1956 projected the scenario of demise that actually happened.

Most people can handle change for the better – a growing market, job promotion, a salary increase, etc. What separates the sheep from the goats is the response to change for the worse – a shrinking market, redundancy, a pay cut, etc. In any organisation, individuals freely come forward to claim responsibility for successes, but when things go wrong a committee is often conveniently assigned the blame. Bad news can induce paralysis or invoke original thinking on a scale seldom witnessed in good times. Necessity really is the mother of invention and companies that reinvent themselves again and again are the ones that make it over the long haul. Motorola, an American electronics giant that was on the ropes because of Japanese competition in conventional fields like colour television, has successfully fought back with a range of new products. These include cellular phones, pagers and two-way radios in the area of mobile communications, and intelligent microprocessors in the area of computers. Motorola has also taken the battle into the enemy's camp by a concerted attempt to corner the Asian market. Nor need the product change radically: clever advertising techniques can keep the image fresh and modern. Coca Cola, Harley Davidson and Xerox are past masters at renewing the image of cool drinks, motorcycles and copiers respectively. Alas, victims as diverse as Pan Am airline and *Punch* magazine failed to discover the magic formula for staying abreast of the changing times. So they expired.

A marvellous contrast of behaviour features the Swiss watch-maker, Société Suisse de Microeléctronique et d'Horlogerie (SSMH), in comparison to the American railway tycoons. In the early 1980s SSMH was nearly wiped out by the cheap digital watch when precision in timing was turned into a cheap, easy-to-reproduce quality by the new quartz technologies. SSMH hit back by introducing the colourful Swatch, focusing on the fashionable youth market while consolidating its position in the top end of the luxury market. The Swatch had fewer parts, which permitted fully automated assembly. This made the watch affordable to youngsters but retained Swiss quality. Over the years Swatches have kept their snazziness because of new lines and limited runs for collectors. The 100 millionth Swatch was recently dispatched. The directors of American railway companies, on the other hand, failed to realise they were in the dying end of the transportation business. Although they had time to build upon their core competencies and branch out into other means of transportation, they stayed with the railroads and their companies died. Ironically, because of traffic congestion and the harm done to the environment by motor cars – Mexico City's ozone level is far above safe limits on most days – mass transportation based on electricity may be on its way back. The trains and trams could come into their own again.

I was asked in an interview what my company might look like in 25 years' time. I replied that if I knew I would be very worried because that would be an indication of stagnation, the fatal disease of large companies. It is much better to have the dynamic tension of the nursery than the deep tranquillity of the graveyard. Employees must always be on their toes. As one said to me: "You're only as good as your last shift."

### Unpredictable Oil and Gold

Futures research is a very risky business. Forecasts can be dreadfully wrong. For this reason economics is sometimes called the "dismal science". Economists are in the habit of underestimating the length and the degree of amplitudes in the business cycle. With a tendency to bunch together in the middle, they are likely to say the boom is over when it isn't and the recovery is at hand when it is still some way away. However, as one of them wryly observed: "To err is human. To be paid to do so is divine!"

One bond trader described the activity of futures research rather well. Charting the future, he said, was like driving down a misty mountain road with no cats' eyes and steep drops into bankruptcy on either side. A technique like scenario planning that improves a company's guidance system should therefore be central to the decision-making process.

A classic example of how scenario planning was used to good effect was the way Royal Dutch Shell reacted swiftly to the second oil price shock of the 1970s. Shell's scenario team had already influenced the mindset of its top decision-makers with imaginative scenarios depicting the unpredictable behaviour of the oil market and in particular the possibility of a major price rise. Shell's plan of action was therefore promptly implemented when the shock came, and put it ahead of its competitors.

More recently the Gulf War demonstrated how much better it is to examine the future with a broad beam of light that may pick up possible turning points and discontinuities, than to try to pinpoint the future with a forecast. Learned studies were circulating before hostilities began that predicted a rise in the oil price to $60 a barrel based on shortages that would develop through dislocations to Middle East supply. In actual fact the price plummeted from $30 to $17 a barrel, prompting a friend of mine to say that oil price forecasters make a flock of sheep look like independent thinkers! They had ignored how much the rest of the world would gear up to compensate for any shortfall.

I hope this example from the oil market convinces you of the high degree of uncertainty permeating the future. Gold is no different. I asked an expert the other day what he thought the price would do. He replied that it could go up or down, but not necessarily in that order! When for general scenario purposes you also have to allow for the inconsistency of politicians – hark back to the quote of the 1960s by Harold Wilson "a week in politics is a long time" – any statement about the future becomes even more fraught with risk. Incredible as it may seem in as rigorous a field as science, an exasperated Albert Einstein once said that God does not play dice. But even such a fine mind as his was proved wrong by the quantum theories of Werner Heisenberg and Erwin Schrödinger. Uncertainty is at the very core of Nature – in the nucleus itself.

## The Probability Trap

One question often put to me is whether mathematical probabilities can be assigned to scenarios. It sounds good but the answer is definitely no. It gives a false sense of precision to what is ultimately a matter of intuitive judgment. The so-called scientific polls conducted before the last South African referendum uniformly underestimated the "yes" vote and the ones before the recent election in the UK even miscalculated the result – a Tory win. Even more short-term is weather forecasting, also considered something akin to a science. But anybody who watched British television on the eve of the gale of October 1987, which caused immense destruction in southeast England, might be forgiven for thinking otherwise. The weatherman's answer to a listener's query about a possible storm was that there was nothing to worry about! Hence, the attaching of specific odds to this or that scenario emerging as correct over-exaggerates the power to predict. To be truthful, you should use qualitative language: this scenario is "likely" or "unlikely", or is "now highly probable" or can be "ruled out".

The world is not a laboratory where you can repeat an experience over and over again to establish a pattern and derive probabilities. History happens once and then it's gone. It's more useful to be vaguely right than precisely wrong. The basic axiom of scenario planning is: accept uncertainty graciously.

## Track Record

In 1985 Anglo pooled its skills with a group of international experts in fields such as population, technology and values to look at what could happen to the world in the 1990s. These experts were incidentally christened "the circle of remarkable people" – and so they proved to be. Against the background of various global scenarios, the political and economic options for South Africa were also examined. When both parts of the study were complete, Anglo very generously allowed me to publish the material and make a series of presentations around South Africa. As one of the scenario team said at the time: "It is one thing to change a company's attitude with scenarios, but a country's – that's something else!"

Here is an extract from the book I wrote in March 1987, *The World and South Africa in the 1990s*. It deals with the requirement for a common vision to help South Africans through the transition:

"The second part of the vision is to negotiate the future with all who will participate in it. The word 'all' should be stressed; we think that there are genuine players from all points of the compass who should be given the opportunity of sitting at the table. We would suggest starting low and aiming high, if one is not to break the crucial condition of equal status around the table. Informal mediation at local, regional and national level could be followed by a SALT-type process whereby professional negotiators are chosen by all the parties concerned to attend a national forum. The leaders are not directly involved at this point. The forum is where most of the detailed negotiations are conducted, with the representatives reporting back and conferring with their respective leaders. The ground having been carefully prepared, the last stage is where the leaders get around the table to finalise the settlement (the parallel being a summit meeting). To start high with the leaders, when so much is at stake, would be fatal. A SALT-type forum gets the right process on the road and overcomes mistrust without posing insurmountable problems to any side." (SALT stands for the Strategic Arms Limitation Talks which were conducted at the time between the United States and the Soviet Union in Switzerland.)

I don't think we could have described the negotiation process in better terms. Since 1985 we have constantly updated our material. In March 1990, in the video *Prospects for the High Road*, I made the following statement about the Soviet Union, some 21 months ahead of its actual dissolution:

"We have one other scenario, which is the disintegration of the Soviet Union, whether it's in a peaceful form or in the form of war. That is another possible scenario."

8

As you can see, that statement is on target too, reflecting the high quality of our futures research. One of our team actually coined the term "Second Reformation" for the period we were studying, on the ground that it might be like the first Reformation that began in 1517 when Martin Luther revolutionised European thinking. And so it has turned out to be – but this time the revolution is all about the collapse of Marxism and the move towards free markets, taking power away from the state and handing it back to the people.

# Structure of the Book

In this new book I am looking farther ahead. What are the major issues in the world facing business as we move into the New Century? Before I tackle them, though, I should explain the structure of the book and how scenario planning works.

*"Rules of the Game"*
Imagine you're a smart Roman in AD zero and you are asked to look 2 000 years ahead. What could you have said with some certainty? Well, you could have said clans will still be around and they will still be fighting one another. You could also have said money will still be in circulation and people will still be trading with one another.

---

**STRUCTURE OF THE BOOK**

*The World*
**Four "rules of the game"**
* **Population**
* **Technology**
* **Social values**
* **"Winning nation" and "winning company"**

**One "key variable"**
* **Relationship between rich and poor nations**

**Two scenarios**
* **"High Road" or "Low Road"?**

*South Africa*
* **Microcosm of the world**
* **"African Dragon" or "Effendi Express"?**
* **Redistribution of skills, not wealth**

---

*Chart 2*

These prognostications would have been based on the assumption that the basic human instincts of kinship, pursuit of power, competitiveness and bartering would continue.

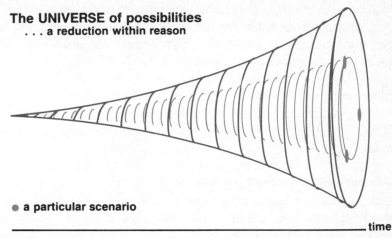

**The UNIVERSE of possibilities**
. . . a reduction within reason

● **a particular scenario**

─────────────────────────────────────────────── time

*Chart 3*

We call these evergreen observations "rules of the game". They are likely to be true whatever the future outcome of the world. There's an old French saying, "*Plus ça change, plus c'est la même chose*", the more things change the more they stay the same. And so it is with the world. The trick in scenario planning is to differentiate those things that stay the same (the rules) from those which are liable to change (the variables). By chance, the new mathematical theory of "chaos" has reached a remarkably similar conclusion. Although the exact course of a chaotic system cannot be predicted, the constraints on its behaviour can be.

We have four rules for the next 20 years: the great divide between the rich and the poor countries and the unprecedented growth in the population of the latter; the revolutionary impact of technology on society; the shift in people's values away from crude materialism to a more balanced approach to life; and the unchanging characteristics of a "winning nation" and a "winning company". These four rules will be covered comprehensively later in the book.

11

### One "Key Variable"

Next we move from the known to the unknown. However much we try to circumscribe the future with "rules of the game", there will be major variables to give an element of uncertainty. The future will always open up as a cone of uncertainty – albeit a narrower one if one is clever with the rules. Just think of what Aids could do to population growth, what fundamentalist Islam could do to geopolitics, or global climate change could do to agriculture. These are all "wild cards" that could change the destiny of the world. From the multitude of uncertainties, we have chosen one "key variable" on which to hinge the scenarios: will the rich nations of this Earth rise to the challenge of assisting the poor to become winners in their own right? Or will they turn their back? It's the critical choice facing mankind today.

### Two Scenarios: "High Road" or "Low Road"?

The third section is about developing the scenarios themselves. The word "scenario" was originally used by Italian composers of opera for the script they wrote summarising the opera's theme. Scripts were circulated to various impresarios to stimulate their interest in producing the opera. The word has been hijacked by the business community to mean a story about a possible future.

We could have produced a whole range of scenarios but instead we concentrated on just two: the "High Road" of closing the gap between the rich and the poor nations, and the "Low Road" of allowing that gap to increase with dire consequences for the stability of the world. As you will see, these scenarios are just as applicable to your country, your community or your company, because each is a group of people with the common interest of achieving economic success. Understanding the big picture helps.

### South Africa: Microcosm of the World

The final section of the book draws attention to the many parallels between the world and South Africa and ends by challenging all South Africans to make a personal contribution towards making the "High Road" happen here. The boulder blocking the path to a better future will not move unless everyone's shoulder is put behind it.

12

## A Special Moment

"So," you may ask, "what is so special about this moment in the world's history that I have to put precious time aside to read the remaining chapters?" The main justification is that the rich nations of the world are at the crossroads after 200 years of virtually uninterrupted industrial progress – other than wars. From now on, progress is no longer guaranteed because there is too much poverty around which can drag the whole system down. That poverty even exists within the rich nations themselves. Worse still, education – the passport to progress – has been deteriorating in some of those nations too, particularly in Britain and America.

Let's go back to the smart Roman in AD zero, to prove how vulnerable progress really is. He might well have looked back on the previous 500 years of Greek and Roman civilisation and been lured into a prophecy that the glorious advance to a higher quality of life would continue undiminished in the world. He would have been

### THE PAST 2 500 YEARS – AND NOW?

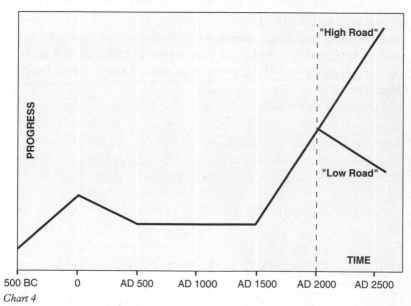

Chart 4

13

wrong. The correct scenario would have gone something like this: the next 500 years will see the decline and ultimate extinction of Roman civilisation. The following 900 years will by and large be a long dark age, after which sudden advances in printing, literature, art and science will trigger another 600 years of progress.

So a "Low Road" for a large portion of the next 2 000 years cannot be discounted for the world. How do we pre-empt this and at least ensure that we take the "High Road" into the 21st Century? Well, for a start, governments everywhere need to appreciate the limited role they can play in the conduct of human affairs. The proverb says: "Govern a great nation like you cook a small fish – don't overdo it!" While all eyes have been on Eastern Europe, the Second Reformation will not be over until the excessive bureaucracy which has grown up in Western countries has also been dismantled.

The principal force that will close the gap between the rich and the poor is the natural desire in most human beings to uplift themselves – given half a chance. Governments are there to release that potential and thereafter step aside. The "High Road" will materialise because the genius of ordinary people, going about their daily lives in a creative manner, ultimately triumphs. That is as true of the world as it is of South Africa.

More than anything, I want you, the readers, to think about our future on this planet; and to anticipate change rather than react to it. Will the New Century be greeted by a "golden dawn" or an "endless night"?

Now is the time to ask.

# 1. Four "Rules of the Game"

First we'll deal with the "rules of the game" for the world.

## Population

The first rule concerns population. We divide the world's population into two parts: the "rich old millions" and the "poor young billions". All generalisations about people are limited because each of us is unique. Yet, of all the divisions in the world today, the most relevant one for our future is that between an acceptable standard of living and no standard of living at all. The current fashion is to talk of "North and South" as though all the above-the-Equator countries are rich and the below-the-Equator countries are poor. It's wrong: the former Soviet Union is part of the "poor young billions", Australia and New Zealand are among the "rich old millions". Moreover, I wanted a classification devoid of racial connotation because there's no intrinsic reason why anybody anywhere should remain poor. For example, racial stereotypes in America conceal one profound consequence of the Civil Rights Act of 1964: 30 per cent of African Americans are middle class.

### "Rich Old Millions"

The "rich old millions" live mainly in the Triad – an ancient Greek term for a group of three. In our case, the core of the Triad comprises Western Europe, Japan and North America. Australia and New Zealand – as mentioned above – are also members, though geographically separate. Outside the Triad lie Eastern Europe and all the republics that formerly constituted the Soviet Union; China and South-East Asia; India; the Middle East; Africa; Central and South America; and numerous independent islands and archipelagos.

The situation should not be considered static, as the Triad has not closed its books to new members. Ones who've recently joined are

**"RICH OLD MILLIONS"**

- **15 per cent of world population but 80 per cent of world production**
- **Income per head 50 times higher than the majority of the "poor young billions"**
- **Live mainly in Triad (US, Japan, Europe)**
- **Population static or declining, therefore geriatric boom**
- **Three regional markets developing: Pacific Rim, Common Market, North American Free Trading Area**
- **Triad integrated through trade and investment**

*Chart 5*

the Asian dragons like Singapore, South Korea, Hong Kong and Taiwan. It does appear, though, that the club never loses its old members: they merely turn into "bobos" – burnt out but opulent.

The world's income is of the order of $20 trillion in today's dollars. The Triad earns about $16 trillion of this total. One can therefore say that the Triad produces 80 per cent of the value of goods and services in the world today, with only 15 per cent of the world's population. Given that there was no divine preference for any nation at the inception of mankind, this is quite a feat. The Triad's average income per head, on an annual basis, is some $20 000 compared with $400 a head for low income economies and $2 400 for middle income economies. Thus there is an income differential of 50:1 between the Triad and the very poor countries and just over 8:1 between the Triad and the middle income group. This compares to national income differentials – taking the ratio of the top 20 per cent of income earners to the bottom 20 per cent – of 4:1 (Sweden) and 9:1 (the US) among rich countries and 5:1 (India) and 33:1 (Brazil) among very poor and middle income countries.

Why worry about the imbalance in the world's income? Apart from the perfectly decent reason of wanting to make the world a better place, one has to be apprehensive about what a high ratio of 50:1

could do to global stability in the next century. As will be seen later on, it is not so much the military threat posed by ultra-poor people to the Triad. If you look back, wars appear to have taken place between countries with small differences in their national per capita incomes, the Gulf War being an exception. The reason for anxiety rests with other links between the rich and the poor nations such as migration. The world, like a nation, is a place where people are constantly comparing their lot with others' – a habit made easier by modern television and radio. This habit breeds a sense of relative deprivation and frustration. Frustrated people have itchy feet.

To add fuel to the fire, the ratio has been rising over the last 20 years because the population growth of the "poor young billions" has ensured that most developing countries have a static or declining per capita income. In a "business-as-usual" projection for the next 50 years, the ratio can therefore be expected to rise even further, while the Triad's population becomes an even smaller minority of world society – around 10 per cent in 2040. Moreover, in our

## DEMOGRAPHY AND INCOME

| | Population Millions | % | Annual per capita income $ | Total income $ Billions | % |
|---|---|---|---|---|---|
| **Low Income Economies** | 3 500 | 64 | 400 | 1 400 | 7 |
| Of which: | | | | | |
| China | 1 100 | 20 | 420 | 460 | 2 |
| India | 900 | 17 | 440 | 400 | 2 |
| **Middle Income Economies** | 1 100 | 21 | 2 400 | 2 600 | 13 |
| **High Income Economies (Triad)** | 800 | 15 | 20 000 | 16 000 | 80 |
| | 5 400 | 100 | 3 700 | 20 000 | 100 |

*Chart 6*

"High Road" scenario to be described later on, it will take many decades for the poorest countries to catch up. For example, if China continues to have an economic growth rate of 10 per cent per annum for the next 25 years, it will come just within reach of the present position of Portugal, Western Europe's poorest country. And China has one-fifth of the world's population.

Let it be said that not all the rich live inside the Triad and not all the poor live outside. Triad cities have their ghettoes, developing countries their upper castes and classes. While the overall measure of income inequality is relatively low in most Triad countries, it hides the lumpy way poverty and wealth tend to be distributed within each country. Desperate inner-city areas are adjacent to comfortable suburbs. Regions of high unemployment stay that way and border more prosperous areas (think of the North versus the South in both England and Italy). Occasionally, as between poles of opposite charge, the tension becomes too great, a spark passes and the poor riot. Although the immediate trigger of the 1992 unrest in Los Angeles was a court decision, the yawning gap between conditions in Beverly Hills and those in South Central Los Angeles must have played a subsidiary role. Nevertheless, to support the earlier point about wars – you fight people close to you – the shops that were worst affected by the rioting were not the ones in the wealthy suburbs but those located in the poor areas themselves, many of them owned by recently arrived Korean immigrants.

So the "rich old millions" who live in the Triad are comparatively rich. Why are they old? Well, the answer is: as you get richer, you have fewer children. You're inclined to regard children as liabilities rather than assets. Private education is expensive and children cramp your lifestyle. You cannot easily go skiing at St Moritz if you've got six children trailing along behind you. Consequently the size of the family falls with growing affluence.

Moreover, Triad women are getting more career conscious. They marry later and they have fewer children. Privately run day-care chains are booming as companies contract out the day care of pre-school children of their female employees. There is even a phenomenon in America called "dinkys" – double income no kids yet couples – where the man and the wife put off having children in their

20s while they pursue their separate "yuppie" careers. Then they have one or two children in their 30s. Almost 70 per cent of US housewives work outside the home; 40 per cent of the US workforce is women. It means that the average size of family in the United States is just over two children. Children are merely replacing their parents. In Japan they talk of "the 1,58 shock". This is because a recent survey showed that the average Japanese housewife has 1,58 children. In Germany and Italy the population is declining. Spain is showing all the symptoms of becoming a wealthy country. The number of children per childbearing woman has dropped from 2,8 in 1975 to 1,4 today; meanwhile the proportion of women aged between 25 and 54 in business and other occupations has risen from 32 per cent in 1982 to 48 per cent in 1991.

### Geriatric Boom

What happens when you have a virtually static or declining population? It ages. All the baby boomers born after the Second World War are now middle-aged boomers, and they're going to be geriatric boomers by the year 2010. It means the hottest market in the United States is not the teenage market of compact discs and Michael Jackson, it's the geriatric market of pharmaceutical drugs and retirement villages. The Japanese were the first to identify this. They are making special "idiot-proof" microwave ovens and video cassette recorders for older people who are not used to the complexities of the Computer Age.

Health is the major issue in the United States. It consumes 12 per cent of Gross National Product. It could rise to 20 per cent of Gross National Product in the first quarter of the next century. People are already asking: how is a static workforce going to look after the burgeoning number of pensioners, and who is going to pay their medical bills?

Dependency ratios – measured in terms of dependants (young and old) per working person – are set to zoom in the Triad in the 21st Century. The proportion of over-65s in the Triad's population will rise from 11 per cent in 1985 to 17 per cent in 2025. In certain countries, such as Switzerland and Japan, this increase will be much higher. In particular, the growth in the population over 85 is set to

19

# HEALTH CARE EXPENDITURES
## AS A PERCENTAGE OF GDP

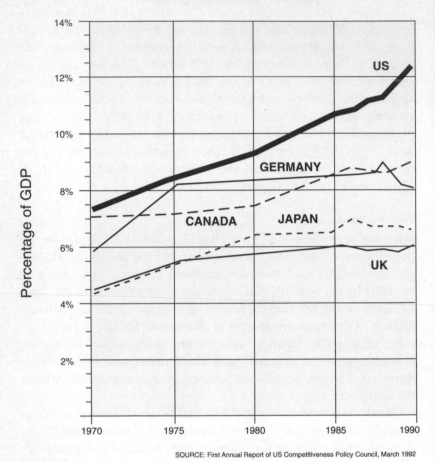

SOURCE: First Annual Report of US Competitiveness Policy Council, March 1992

*Chart 7*

be even more rapid than for the elderly as a whole. As for centenarians, there are now almost 36 000 in the US and this figure is expected to rise to more than one million by 2080. Perhaps the figure could be even higher if life-lengthening drugs are available in the not too distant future. A century will then be retirement age!

One can expect a stronger political will in the Triad to limit inflation, because governments will more and more have to listen to

# DEPENDENCY RATIOS

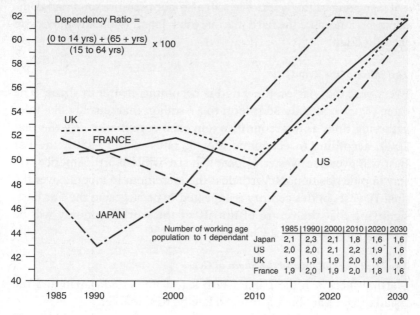

Dependency Ratio =

$$\frac{(0 \text{ to } 14 \text{ yrs}) + (65 + \text{yrs})}{(15 \text{ to } 64 \text{ yrs})} \times 100$$

| Number of working age population to 1 dependant | 1985 | 1990 | 2000 | 2010 | 2020 | 2030 |
|---|---|---|---|---|---|---|
| Japan | 2,1 | 2,3 | 2,1 | 1,8 | 1,6 | 1,6 |
| US | 2,0 | 2,0 | 2,1 | 2,2 | 1,9 | 1,6 |
| UK | 1,9 | 1,9 | 1,9 | 2,0 | 1,8 | 1,6 |
| France | 1,9 | 2,0 | 1,9 | 2,0 | 1,8 | 1,6 |

*Chart 8*

the demands of the elderly as they make up a greater share of the electorate. Physical security and the maintenance of law and order will be high on the agenda too. Even now, retirement villages are beginning to look like the walled cities of medieval times. Triad companies will find that the cost of maintaining their pension funds and medical aid schemes in a financially sound state will figure significantly in the overall cost of their products and services. This may serve to erode their competitive position vis-à-vis companies in younger non-Triad nations. Inevitably, more pressure will be exerted on people during their working lives to set money aside themselves for their old age. Taxes on income from such savings may be reduced or eliminated in order to encourage such a trend.

Magazines are changing their content and designers their fashions as the big bulge of female baby boomers enters the ranks of middle age. The "stay for ever young and eternally slim" philosophy is making way for straight talk about how to overcome the problems of ageing and get the most enjoyment out of one's later years.

The ageing of the workforce will also put pressure on Triad companies to automate the hard manual jobs. Japan is already moving in that direction.

### The Shape of the Triad

Every year that passes, the Triad is becoming clearer in shape. The three regions, already $6 trillion to $7 trillion markets, are like trees gathering rings as new countries join each core market. By the year 2000, according to economic growth rates of the 1980s, the Far East will overtake Western Europe in size while North America will stay in pole position. Nevertheless the increment in income over the final 10 years of this century is expected to be largest in the Far East, signifying that the centre of gravity of the world economy will be moving there in the 21st Century.

### The First Leg: Japan and the Skein of Geese

Starting then with the Far Eastern leg of the Triad, Japan and the Asian dragons are busy forming a Pacific Rim market.

However, membership of this market is widening. In addition to the four dragons of Singapore, South Korea, Hong Kong and Taiwan, other incoming members include Malaysia, Thailand, Indonesia and the Philippines. Noticeably, the foreign direct investment by the four dragons is rivalling Japan's investment in the economies of the new members. As wages rise in the successful economies, every company is seeking to locate part of its manufacturing base offshore in countries where labour is still inexpensive. Indeed, investment is cascading down to the lowest-cost nations fairly swiftly as technology is easily transferable.

Crucially, the gigantic labour pool of China is only beginning to be utilised. Many Chinese companies in Hong Kong have moved part of their operations to the Guangdong province of China adjoining Hong Kong. With its 65 million people, Guangdong has averaged 12 per cent per annum economic growth over the last 10 years. The Chinese government has given far more economic freedom to the southern coastal provinces of China (Guangdong, Fujian and

Hainan) than to the interior, with the result that they're flourishing now. Consequently China's ailing state sector has fallen from 80 per cent of its Gross National Product in the early 1980s to about 50 per cent in 1992. As one Hong Kong businessman put it: "I've done business in Guangdong for longer than I can remember and I haven't met a Communist yet." To support this statement, about one million people travelled to the southern town of Shenzhen in August 1992 for a chance to buy new shares on the Shenzhen stock exchange. Riots broke out when many people were turned away empty-handed. Honda has recently announced that it intends to produce motorcyles in China, which may herald an invasion of China by Japanese companies.

One of our scenario team likened the coming-together of the Far East to a skein of geese flying in "V" formation with Japan at the head of the "V". Gradually, more geese join. Vietnam is mooted to be the latest member. It possesses inhabitants widely known for their self-sacrifice and dedication to hard work. It also has a National Scientific Research Centre noted for its mathematical skills and its attempts to improve Vietnamese agriculture. Positions of individual members in the "V" change and the "V" itself widens or narrows as countries catch up or fall behind Japan. On the whole, though, whereas Japan forged ahead on its own in the last 30 years, its continuing excellence will more and more be attributable to the synergy which goes with being a member of a group of high-flying geese. It is not beyond the realms of possibility that by the middle of the next century Japan's relationship with China will be very much like Britain's present relationship with America, but without the cultural affinity. Perversely, the country that is among the laggards is the one that has received most American help – the Philippines.

Not everyone in Japan likes what is going on. There is talk of the "hollowing-out" of Japanese industry as manufacturing jobs move overseas and Japan is left with white collar occupations. But the relentless drive by Japanese companies to bring costs down in order to remain competitive in the world will ensure that the process of relocation is unstoppable. Australian companies are following suit as wages in Australia are sometimes 100 times those of countries to the north.

### The Second Leg: The Common Market: Widening or Deepening?

Moving next to the European leg of the Triad, we have an interesting set of scenarios. Essentially there are two models that Europe could follow. The one involves deepening the relationship between the existing Community members to the extent that a confederal/federal structure will be in place by the year 2000, possibly heading for a "United States of Europe". The European Parliament in Brussels will be the focus of European authority. A loose relationship will be maintained with Eastern European countries, Russia, the Ukraine and the other republics of the former Soviet Union.

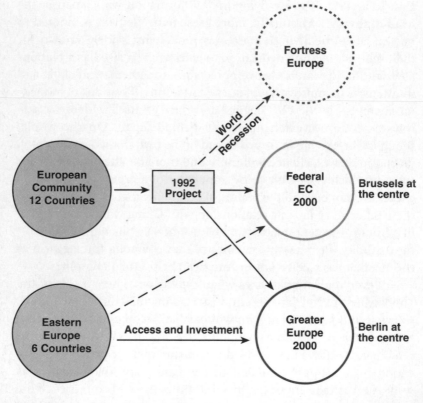

## SCENARIOS FOR EUROPE

*Chart 9*

The other model sees the minimum of centralised bureaucracy required to maintain an open Common Market with the widening of that market to include Scandinavian, Central European and Eastern European countries by the year 2000. The net may even be cast further to include the Ukraine and perhaps Russia itself. In this event, the balance of European power might veer eastward to Berlin.

The two models are not incompatible, and moves to deepen and widen relationships between European countries may be made at the same time. Nevertheless, obstacles tending to slow down either process are legion. On the one hand, Britain in particular does not wish to surrender the level of political sovereignty it would be necessary to forgo to join a federation. The Danes have in June 1992 shown their divided feelings in a referendum in which they rejected the Maastricht Treaty on European union by a wafer-thin majority. On the other hand, France and others do not want cheap East European iron and steel, textiles and agricultural products to flood the Common Market. Moreover, the staggering cost so far borne by 63 million West Germans to uplift 17 million East Germans does not augur well for co-operation between the West and the East. Transfers from West to East Germany amounted to $84,5 billion in 1991 and are expected to be $110 billion in 1992. Some of this amount is being funded through taxes but most of it is financed by increased public borrowings. The stakes are high, because a Greater Europe, including Russia, could incorporate another $1,5 trillion of Gross National Product – making it the largest of the three Triad markets.

### The Third Leg: America: North and South

An interesting mixture is emerging in the third leg of the Triad. The US is edging closer to Canada and Mexico to form the North American Free Trading Area (NAFTA). Again, forces are at work to thwart this development. At the best of times the relationship between Canada and the US is delicate because of Canadian anxieties about being overwhelmed by the giant next door. In a recession, trade becomes an even touchier subject because of loss of jobs on either side of the border caused by cheaper goods exported from the other.

Mexico, with its much lower labour costs, is considered an even greater threat to US industry by US unions. The explosion of business on the Mexican side of the border, fuelled mainly by US companies relocating labour-intensive operations there, lends substance to the arguments of the unionists. Equally, many environmentalists are up in arms about the damage along the border caused by the unrestrained growth of industry. Yet the potential for a common market to the south is huge with Mexico acting as a gateway to Central and South America. Chile has already asked whether it can join NAFTA.

### Triad Integration

The three legs of the Triad are also being drawn together by the mutual advantages of international trade. In the last 10 years, both North America's and Western Europe's trade with the Pacific Rim has been growing at over 10 per cent per annum, a figure similar to the annual increase within the Pacific Rim itself. All the intra-Triad trade figures have compounded faster than the 5 per cent overall increase in world trade. This implies that Triad companies have a better idea of what sells in other Triad markets than non-Triad companies do.

World-class companies such as Sony, Toyota, IBM and Coca-Cola have subsidiaries or associates in each leg of the Triad. They want to be close to their customers, and they want to avoid trade barriers by being inside each market. They are cementing the relationship between Triad countries. Pity outsiders to the Triad who want to compete against these companies. Firstly, their home market is usually not of a sufficient size to achieve the economies of scale necessary to lower unit costs to a level where they can play in the same ball game as the Triad giants. Secondly, outsiders don't have the sensitive antennae to the volatile changes in consumer taste that Triad insiders possess – they're not as fleet-footed. Thirdly, outsiders don't have the international manufacturing network which wrings the last cent out of each country's comparative advantage. Triad car companies now assemble their models from components made throughout the world. Fourthly, outsiders normally don't come close to the after-sales service of Triad giants because they lack the density of marketing outlets on the ground. In other words, as an outsider you have to have a product or service which is unique or of almost unbelievable quality or eye-blinkingly cheap to make headway against the traditional brands of Triad companies within their own markets.

Foreign direct investment (FDI) made by companies resident in America, Japan, Germany, Britain and France (the G5) in other countries became a flood in the 1980s, amounting to $650 billion for the decade. The opening of the gates was partially due to the liberalisation of service industries like banking, insurance, tele-communications and tourism. However, three-quarters of that $650 billion went to other G5 countries. By the end of 1989, companies in these five countries owned nearly $2 trillion of assets abroad. Japanese firms especially went on a binge, building car factories in Britain, buying prestigious properties like the Rockefeller Centre in New York as well as acquiring golf courses (including Pebble Beach) and a large slice of the Hollywood film industry. In Australia, most of the Queensland "Gold Coast" and the majority of hotels there are now in Japanese hands. It caused a Queenslander to remark: "In the old days you sent in an army to conquer a country with weapons and generals, and you fought boring things called battles. Nowadays you put a businessman on a 747 with a plastic card, and he buys the country. The result's the same. The Japanese wouldn't have at-tacked Pearl Harbor these days: they'd have bought it."

If Triad integration via mutual investment continues at the same pace, it will make a mockery of international trade flows. Medium-sized and even small Triad companies are joining the overseas in-vestment bandwagon. Once foreign firms have established them-selves in a new host market, their local purchases of supplies and sales to customers are equivalent to imports and exports. For the US and Japan, trade between foreign-based firms and their host markets is equivalent to around half of the external trade flows between the two countries. In addition, both Japanese and American companies contribute significantly to the external trade figures through "intra-company" transfers, where a principal ships goods to a subsidiary overseas or vice versa. It is thought that two-thirds of all American imports from Japan are shipped "intra-company" and nearly half the other way. Much of the latter, though, come from Japanese-owned subsidiaries in the United States who in aggregate are the largest American source of exports to Japan.

An amusing incident in the US points the way to the "New World Order". A municipality wishing to demonstrate its support of the "put America first" programme bought a tractor with an American badge at a higher price than a tractor with a Japanese badge. The only problem was that the former was actually put together in Japan and the latter in the US!

Two-thirds of the total world stock of foreign assets relating to FDI is held by just three countries – the US, UK and Japan. Together with France and Germany, these five account for over three-quarters of FDI flows. Showing how difficult it is for countries outside the Triad to entice Triad companies to invest in them, the absolute amount of FDI into developing countries was lower in real terms in the 1980s than in the 1970s. But the Asian dragons were luckier: Triad investment in them increased. In 1991 the Asian region accounted for 60 per cent of FDI inflows into developing countries, compared to 27 per cent between 1975 and 1979. It bears out the truth of the statement "to the victor, the spoils".

The cherry on the top for Triad integration is the regular meeting of its "executive committee". It is called the Group of Seven or G7, being the G5 – the US, Germany, the UK, Japan and France – plus Canada and Italy. It affords a wonderful opportunity for each world leader to be photographed with his or her peers. Communiques are issued with much pomp and ceremony to the media afterwards.

### *"Poor Young Billions"*

Now we contrast the Triad with the rest of the world in which the overwhelming majority of the "poor young billions" live. The world population in 1988 was 5 billion. It will be 6 billion in the year 2000 and 7 billion in the year 2012. We're compressing into 12 years what it took three million years to create the first time – one billion people. India produces Australia every year in numbers (17 million people) and yet it has only one-third the area of the United States. Even if India manages to halve its average size of family from four where it is today to two by 2030, its population will continue to grow until

**"POOR YOUNG BILLIONS"**

\* **Additional one billion people every 12 years**
\* **Slowdown in population growth not predetermined**
\* **Megacities of 20 million in Third World**
\* **"Effendis" largely to blame for poverty**
\* **But turnaround in Mexico and Argentina**
\* **Population bomb or market of the future?**

*Chart 10*

the end of the next century. By that time India's population will be 2 billion, the same as the world's in 1925.

Sub-Saharan Africa (558 million people) produces Ghana (16 million people) every year. Despite a death rate of 14 persons per 1 000 per annum against a world average of 9 per 1 000, and a life expectancy of 52 years against a world average of 63 years (52 was the world's figure 30 years ago), sub-Saharan Africa still has one of the highest population growth rates in the world at 3,1 per cent per annum. The reason is simply an annual birth rate of 45 babies per 1 000 versus a world average of 26. Aids, to which I refer in more detail later on, is sure to depress Africa's future population growth rate but it is still far from clear by how much the figure will fall and when. Drought has always been part of Africa's cycle. Recognising Africa's erratic climate, farmers a few centuries ago were nomadic. When it didn't rain they moved on. Numbers have now made farming a sedentary occupation. If it doesn't rain, you're lucky if you can claim some government relief.

Returning to world population growth, one can quickly do the calculation that an extra one billion people every 12 years is just over 83 million additional people per year. Over half the increase is contributed by India, China and sub-Saharan Africa. Although it is absurd to extrapolate over 1 000 years, at the present rate the world's population would be 90 billion in AD 3000. However, the reason for saying this is that it is equally arbitrary – or an act of wishful thinking – to state, as many worthy demographers do, that the world's popu-

29

# EVOLUTION OF WORLD POPULATION

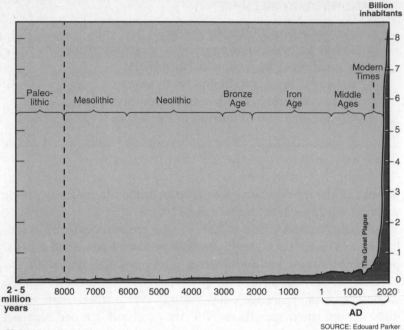

*Chart 11*

SOURCE: Edouard Parker

lation will level out in the latter half of the 21st Century at around 12 billion. Yes, fertility rates around the world are falling at the moment, which suggests an equilibrium state at some stage in the future. Yes, rising per capita income does tend to bring down family size, particularly if it is allied to an effective network of family planning advice bureaux and to equal educational opportunities for women so that having children is a democratic decision between husband and wife. But no, it is not predetermined that fertility rates will fall to a point where zero world population growth is assured, because the majority of people may become poorer, not richer, and further advances in medicine may dramatically increase the life span of the poor. It must also be said that, mathematically, as the absolute number of people in the world increases, so the population growth rate has to decline gradually in percentage terms to yield a constant increment of 83 million people a year. In other words, we are already postulating falling birth rates in the world when we talk of projecting 83 million a year *ad infinitum*.

Extraneous shocks, heaven forbid, could do what a natural decline in fertility rates cannot. A nuclear winter after a nuclear war, Aids or some other virus, starvation caused by a shortage of water or desertification, an encounter with an asteroid – any of these could dramatically reduce, stop or reverse population growth.

Advocates of strict birth control measures maintain that it is totally irresponsible to rely on either the "flattening out" prediction of demographic experts or surprises of the kind mentioned above. They want intervention – now – in the form of fiscal disincentives for having more than one or two children. Each additional child will attract a "living fee". At the same time, they demand that contraceptives and sterilisation be made easily available and affordable. Ultimately, some of them argue, the United Nations will be compelled to impose sanctions on any country exceeding certain preordained ceilings on population growth, when environmental damage becomes extreme and is traced back to sheer numbers of people.

For most of us, direct intervention of this nature represents a most offensive invasion of personal liberty. How many babies a family has is a private affair between man and wife. Furthermore, there are racial overtones because the thrust of any campaign to curb population growth will inevitably be aimed at the poor, not the rich. But the practice of issuing universal directives in defence of the environment has already been established.

Chlorofluorocarbons are being phased out by the mid-to-late 1990s under the Montreal Protocol and man may have to use less of his first invention – fire – if the "greenhouse" lobby has its way in reducing dependence on fossil fuels. Nonetheless, it's a quantum leap to move from protocols limiting the use of raw materials by developed countries to ones limiting the creation of life by the developing ones.

How would our smart Roman have reacted to the idea of 5 billion people on this planet? Probably in the same way that we react to the concept of 90 billion in the year 3000. Impossible!

Megacities are mushrooming. Mexico City and São Paulo have more than 20 million inhabitants each, raising unprecedented problems of housing, of traffic congestion, of pollution. Indeed, the Mexican government has closed an oil refinery in the centre of Mexico City because of respiratory problems found in children. Cars are banned one day a week in the city, in order to reduce the level of pollution in the city air which is well beyond acceptable limits on most days.

The Mexican minister of the environment has been informally renamed "minister of winds" because people wish he had the power to summon the winds to blow the pollution away. The president of Mexico, Carlos Salinas De Gortari, recently estimated that the cost of improving the air in Mexico City is more than $4,5 billion. "We are paying a very high price for having neglected the environment in the past," he said.

For most well-to-do people, the only window on the way the poor live in the megacities of the Third World is the odd item in the media or an occasional visit on holiday or business. Even then, in the latter case, the glimpse is usually through the lens of a luxury international hotel and the scene is the smart part of town. The cultural flux of these vast metropolises undermines the old structures of identity and affinity present in the family and small villages. The social fabric breaks down. One sociologist provided a frightening analogy: "It's as though all the spider webs in the jungle had been destroyed by shifting winds. And the spiders scuttle aimlessly about the ground." National records cannot be kept of such a huge, precarious population. It lies outside the control, or even the awareness of, formal political and economic institutions.

The bad news abounds. Crime is rife. Kids steal, kids sleep out, kids are slaves, kids get murdered. Life is cheap. Water is risky, medicines are fake. Schools are war zones. Corruption is endemic. But the locals still have a sense of humour, calling their hospitals "departure lounges" and their shops "queue-wait". Mass transit systems are so inefficient that people are exhausted by the time they get home from work. On the job their productivity suffers through straight fatigue. Women are the stars, many bringing up children alone and working to pay the household bills – putting the menfolk to shame with their longer hours.

In Bogotá in Colombia, a daily hearse collects unidentified bodies from the morgue and ferries them to the graveyard for a mass blessing by the local priest. No birth certificate, no death certificate – life unrecorded. In another South American city BMWs are German "take-aways" so that old "skins" are put on new chassis to disguise their age. Advice to tourists is: "Don't be a pedestrian. Take a taxi to cross the street. But if you happen to be a pedestrian in a thick smog and you're being followed, bend right down to look at the shoes to establish the pursuer's whereabouts. Visibility is clear for six inches above the pavement."

The litany of woe is endless in these massive urban clusters of the developing world. But the good news is that against all odds they also produce outstanding heroes and champions. Teachers, social workers, entrepreneurs, entertainers, priests, sportsmen and -women – their hunger to make a personal contribution to society frequently eclipses the ambitions of their silver-spooned counterparts in the Triad. Interestingly, many Triad cities used to have the same destitute conditions (some still do in parts). Not so long ago London was known to its inhabitants as the Infernal Wen. "Wen" means a wart. In fact my great-great-aunt Beatrice Webb raised the awareness of the British public to the ghastly conditions of the East End of London at the beginning of this century.

### The Effendis

Why are the "poor young billions" young? Well, nearly half of most developing countries' populations are under 15 years old. Furthermore, 90 per cent of the world's under-15s will reside in developing countries in the year 2005. Why are they poor? Most developing countries cannot grow their economies faster than their populations. There are one or two exceptions – the Asian dragons, Chile in South America, Botswana in Africa. But why so many failures when people are naturally talented?

The answer is that they have been badly served by their rulers. The majority of "poor young billions" are under the thrall of the "Effendis", a name given to the educated class by Edouard Parker, a member of our "circle of remarkable people". It was, you may re-call, a Turkish title of respect chiefly applied to officials and profes-sional men. In this context it is applied in a less praiseworthy sense: the Effendi is the fellow who knows it all. Consider – there are more educated people in the world than ever before. They are a force for positive or negative change. Unfortunately, most Effendis fall into the latter category because, as intellectuals, they have an inborn ten-dency to want to interfere in the lives of the common people in order to put them on the right track. This interference is usually counter-productive even if the intentions are excellent. For the common man or woman has a far better idea of where his or her own interests lie than an Effendi has. It is what Friedrich von Hayek called the "fatal conceit".

Effendis of the negative kind have four principal drawbacks: they constitute an unaffordable expense for most poor countries, many of them being funded out of taxpayers' money; they are meddlesome, issuing time-delaying regulations and directives that clog up the pri-vate sector (in many instances having inherited all the worst admin-istrative instincts of the previous colonial power); they are long on impractical development theories usually picked up at one of the "progressive" Western universities, and short on experience in the field; and they never speak of trade-offs, believing that life is one long list of entitlements to be satisfied out of a bottomless financial pot. It is worth recalling that Africa, particularly sub-Saharan Afri-ca, was a viable social unit before great administrative superstruc-tures were piled onto the basic village network. When the colonial powers departed, the cost of these superstructures was suddenly swung onto the local population (having in large measure previously been borne overseas). Moreover, the newly independent countries were saddled with the worst of Western ideologies, as naturally the new Effendis – colloquially named Wabenzis for their predilection for German luxury cars – picked those which consolidated their positions of power.

Some would contend that the United States has gone through a similar experience: from its great pioneering days of the last cen-tury to the present malaise under the Washington Effendis. The only difference is that you cannot blame the US experience on a colonial power. Other Western countries too have their citadels of "Effendi-dom."

The instinctive reaction of an Effendi is to veto rather than support, to procrastinate rather than decide. He considers the airing of opposing views unnecessary, and calls for consensus and unity based on "the will of the people" – in reality on his own terms. He loftily dismisses anyone who espouses classical liberal ideals as out of date and naïve. He will often exaggerate how bad things are in the world to justify his making a personal intervention to rectify the situation. You will find a typical Effendi sitting in an airconditioned office in a Third World capital in learned discourse with an international expert on the latest trends in agro-economics, when people are starving to death within kilometres of the capital. He will build universities when the country is crying out for basic literacy and practical skills training. He spurns foreign investment and skilled immigrants because both are threats to his power base. If you confront an Effendi with his dismal track record, the standard excuse is that the misery is entirely due to neo-colonialism or to the rapaciousness of multinationals. He never explains how some poor countries have done exceedingly well under the identical conditions of the world economic game; nor how some communities – the Chinese, Indian and Jewish communities, to name but three – appear to flourish so well in foreign lands. Could it be that they live beyond the reach of the Effendis at home?

Perhaps the saddest aspect of the whole Effendi saga is that their interventionist inclinations have been fully supported by the "progressive" school in literature. Influential authors and poets have time and again romanticised the dirigiste systems of government that allow too much power at the centre and thereby cause the appalling conditions of the "poor young billions". As free spirits, they have advocated undemocratic philosophies that enslave other men and women and systemically deny them the opportunity to fulfil themselves as individuals. They silently pass over how central planning has destroyed the ecology of the Soviet Union – polluting the clear waters of Lake Baikal, the world's deepest fresh-water lake, desiccating the Aral Sea in pursuit of cotton, turning the Volga into a sewer. Instead they focus all their criticism on the capitalist system which, though admittedly imperfect and therefore improved by some of the criticism, has delivered the prosperity of the Industrial Age. Anointed by the media and academia alike, these authors and poets are responsible for the "Great Literary Fraud" of the 20th Century.

The challenge is how do we turn the Effendis into a force for positive change, as they are the most influential class in developing countries? How do we get them to step back when their instinct is to step forward? For therein lies the solution that will transform the vicious circle of rising poverty and larger families into a virtuous circle of increasing affluence bringing down family size.

Well, it's already happening. For the first time in countries like Mexico and Argentina, the Effendis are on the side of those who wish to cut back on State bureaucracies and the role of government. They support the notion of a thriving private sector and the concept of private property. The prevailing *zeitgeist* among these Effendis is that any intervention of a fiscal or monetary nature must be intended to help business flourish. So the clouds of bureaucracy are parting and in the warm rays of deregulation millions of microbusinesses are being nurtured to fulfil the everyday demands of consumers. The "informals" are no longer considered mere refugees from the formal sector of the economy. They are one of the essential driving forces behind the "High Road" scenario. Moreover, word of the successful formula for becoming a Latin dragon is spreading fast throughout Central and South America. And thank heavens, the Effendis on other continents are stirring to the new ideas.

Let's illustrate with some figures how exciting the last point is. If the 1990s is a repeat of the 1980s, the lion's share of the total increment in global income during the current decade will remain with the Triad. This picture, however, would change dramatically if non-Triad per capita income growth were to accelerate to 5 per cent or 7 per cent per annum as is perfectly possible in principle. Then the increments of Triad and non-Triad would be similar. But the real kicker occurs in the next century, assuming a "High Road" evolution. Population growth is expected to be effectively zero in the Triad over the period 2000 to 2025 in contrast to a strong 1,7 per cent annual rate in developing countries. The combination of higher per capita income growth with consistently higher population growth would result in developing countries accounting for the greater part of world economic growth.

At this stage I can see some readers being somewhat puzzled by the ambiguity of the analysis. On the one hand, should they liken the "poor young billions" to a population bomb that has already been detonated with irreversible consequences for Mother Earth? On the other hand, aren't the "poor young billions" in the vanguard of the "High Road" – the people and the market of the future? Yet this is exactly the kind of ambivalence a reader should feel because it provides an inkling of the two possible roads ahead: what I termed the "critical choice facing mankind today".

### One World

We all live in one world. If you are an astronaut orbiting the Earth in a space shuttle and you look down, you see that we live on this tiny

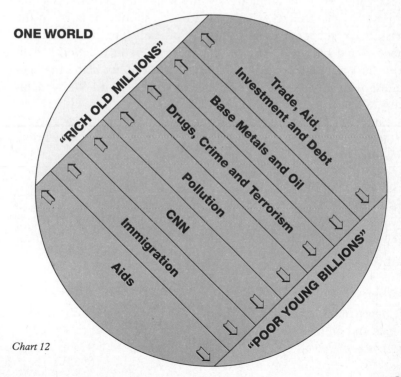

*Chart 12*

37

blue ball in the freezing void of space. On this ball, surrounded by a unique but fragile envelope of atmospheric gases, the "rich old millions" and the "poor young billions" are locked in an inescapable embrace. Neither side can blast off in a rocket ship to another planet. Everyone is here to stay. What then are the unbreakable links between the two?

### World Economy

We have economic links: trade, aid, investment and a Third World debt now valued at $1 trillion. As has already been remarked, international trade and investment have grown fastest within the Triad, i.e. as a result of rich-rich transactions. Growth in rich-poor and poor-poor trade and investment has been far less spectacular and in some cases has actually been negative. The dangers in creating a two-speed world of "separate development" are obvious.

Aid is no longer doled out the way it used to be either. The rich nations are wary of pouring money into what they perceive as a bottomless pit, particularly when much of the money ends up in the Swiss bank accounts of government officials presiding over the "poor young billions". Anyway capital is short in the world these days, the only nation with a fair degree of liquidity being the Taiwanese with a war chest of $84 billion. As to Third World debt, many Western banks originally lending the money have either written much of it off (the euphemistic expression is "debt forgiveness") or offloaded it to other parties at a heavy discount on face value. Nevertheless, the overdrafts of some developing countries are still of a sufficient magnitude for the banks to maintain an intense interest in the fate of the borrowers. Samuel Johnson once said: "A loan is a gift until it is repaid." Having had their fingers burnt, the banks of the rich are now making further commitments only to those "poor young billions" from whom repayments of interest and principal are forthcoming.

### Resources

We have resource linkages. Japan in particular is dependent on base metals and oil from the Third World, although it tries to spread its sources as widely as possible. In 1988 Japan imported 93 per cent of

38

the world's exported nickel ore, 57 per cent of exported copper ore and 30 per cent of coal and iron.

## The Underworld

Drugs, crime, terrorism – that's the sleazy, demonic link. You only have to think of the drug trade from South America into the United States. For all the American assistance in the form of men and matériél to South American governments to wipe out the sources of cocaine and other substances, the powder still gets through the net. Too many of the "rich old millions" are hooked. While the demand is there and prices are high, the trade will never stop. Crime is an international business, drugs are the most lucrative export. It is estimated that the 24 Mafia families in the US make at least $60 billion a year (gross and net). Their turf is increasingly being invaded by new Hispanic and Asian networks.

The terrorist link is no better demonstrated than by the tragedy of Pan Am Flight 103 which fell out of the sky onto Lockerbie in Scotland on December 21st, 1988. The "rich old millions" are using every means at their disposal to see that justice is done. One hopes that had the plane been full of "poor young billions", justice would have been pursued equally relentlessly. It need hardly be said that in our "High Road" scenario, the life of a "poor young billion" is equal in worth to the life of a "rich old million".

## The Environment

Another undesirable bridge between the "rich old millions" and the "poor young billions" is pollution. A stark reminder is the unpleasant news for West Europeans that plenty of the old Chernobyl-type nuclear reactors are still in operation in the former Soviet Union and Eastern Europe. Other differently designed reactors there are not up to Western standards of safety either. For example, foreign experts are urging the Bulgarian government to shut down its four reactors as soon as possible. There can be no worse international pollution threat than radioactive dust, something which the nuclear energy programmes of the French and Japanese have precluded with superior safety features.

One country's emission is another country's acid rain. We're cre-

39

**THE ENVIRONMENT**

- * **Nearly an acre of forest lost per second**
- * **10,5 per cent of world's fertile land degraded**
- * **Water becoming a precious commodity**
- * **Industrialisation of Third World a threat**
- * **Conserve in return for cash**

*Chart 13*

ating three more people per second. In that same second we are cutting down almost an acre of tropical forest somewhere in the world, dumping nearly 500 tons of greenhouse gases into the atmosphere and discharging some 800 tons of topsoil, fertilisers, pesticides and industrial wastes into the oceans. And we're losing, it is thought, 10 species of fauna and flora every day.

The global figures are truly frightening. Since 1945, 1,2 billion hectares of land have suffered moderate to extreme degradation accounting for 10,5 per cent of the planet's fertile land. Some 25 billion tons of topsoil are lost each year through soil erosion caused by overgrazing by livestock, inefficient farming practices and deforestation. In Central America 24 per cent of the land is damaged, in Africa 14 per cent and in North America a more moderate 4,4 per cent. However, it is no exaggeration to say that we are beginning to turn the Earth into a lunar landscape – and we have nowhere else in the universe to go. Moreover, overfishing is doing unknown damage to the world beneath the waves. Falling catches in Iceland and elsewhere provide indirect evidence of the rapid depopulation of Neptune's kingdom.

Water is turning into a commodity more sought after than a precious metal. We've taken water for granted for thousands of years, it's been freely available like air. No longer. As we strive to feed ever greater numbers of humanity, more and more water is used for irrigation. Three-quarters of the fresh water worldwide is used as such and in the poorest countries 90 per cent. Unfortunately the Green Revolution, as the massive increase in crop production on irrigated land in India and other developing countries is called, is beginning to show harmful side-effects. The deposition of salts on the surface and in the topsoil at root level is rendering the land infertile. One-quarter of the total irrigated land in the world has been adversely affected in this way (the proportion in India is put at 36 per cent). Irrigation has run into the law of diminishing returns.

Environmentalists, therefore, are calling for a commercial and not a subsidised price to be applied to water for farming purposes. In this way it should be allocated more rationally across all uses as it becomes scarcer. Mighty rivers like the Euphrates and the Nile are becoming potential sources of conflict among the nations that draw their water from them. Moreover, weather patterns may be changing as a result of global warming, some countries becoming wetter, others drier. Water – the essential life-giving substance – could be the ultimate bond tying the rich to the poor.

Between the intense consumerism of the Triad and the sheer numbers and poverty of the Third World, the environment is already struggling to survive. But what will happen if the "poor young billions" decide to follow the same path to industrialisation as the "rich old millions"? To raise the real incomes of the developing countries near to the present levels enjoyed by the Triad will – with present technologies – entail a dramatic increase in their per capita consumption of energy and other pollution-causing commodities. If China, as it plans to, eventually doubles its coal consumption to two billion tons a year, what will this do to the air breathed in Tokyo? Such an action will dwarf the carbon-saving measures of Western countries.

The trouble is that it costs money to adopt environmentally friendly paths to industrialisation. Scrubbers that remove sulphurous gases from the stacks of coal-burning power stations do not come cheap. China will argue that its competitiveness will be damaged if it cannot use its vast coal resources as it chooses. Brazil and Indonesia are already extremely touchy about other countries interfering in the way they exploit their tropical forests. It is hard for the Triad to make a case for preserving the last two-thirds of the original forest cover of the Earth on the ground that it is the greatest potential gene pool for future medicines, when at the same time Triad companies are placing their next orders for furniture, plywood and newspaper pulp. Apart from the inconsistency, the prospect of immediate foreign exchange will, from a financial point of view, always be more attractive to the owner of the forests than some hypothetical gain from some still-to-be-discovered pharmaceutical drug. That is unless a giant like Merck comes along with cash for "chemical prospecting" rights as it has done in Costa Rica, enabling the country to set aside a quarter of its land – with possibly half a million species – for conservation. On a lowlier scale, how do you persuade landless peasants struggling to survive not to clear the next acre of forest, because it diminishes the Earth's capacity to convert carbon dioxide into oxygen? How do you tell them the forest floor is not suitable for cultivation or grazing: the soil will be exhausted within one or two years and then nothing will grow? "Slash and burn" keeps bodies warm and bellies full for another day.

Tourism is often held up as a strong economic justification for safeguarding Nature. There again one senses something phoney about this approach, as many of the places are inaccessible to the average suburban Triad family. Moreover, even if they are accessible tourism can do irreversible damage to the environment as in the Swiss Alps where 40 million annual visitors tramp around the slopes and 40 000 ski runs scar the mountainside.

The Triad is beginning to realise that for every time "green" logic and economics converge to make a decision easy, there is an equivalent number of examples where they depart from one another. Frequently, "green" good entails economic pain. Nature has to be preserved – period. The protection of the world's plants and animals and the maintenance of a stable global climate are ends in themselves. Where a decision to pursue these ends goes against the market, money has to be found to compensate the developing countries which can ill afford to sub-optimise their economic growth rates (a global figure of $125 billion a year has been mentioned). This is the basis of the proposals put forward by the poor countries at the Earth Summit in Rio de Janeiro in June 1992. They want the Triad to recycle to them a portion of its 80 per cent of world income as compensation for ceasing to exploit assets of worldwide environmental significance. Conserve in return for cash, or "debt forgiveness": it would be a crude but effective start in a decade when lobbies on behalf of the environment, and public concern about all environmental issues, are sure to grow.

Nonetheless, this type of initiative must not disguise the fact that many of the environmental problems of the Third World may be resolved through education, better administration and moderate amounts of capital. For example, the supply of clean drinking water, simple ways of dealing with sewage and the protection of topsoil are nearer to the hearts of disadvantaged communities than the maintenance of biodiversity.

### Global Communication

CNN is creating a global electronic village. One country is instantly aware now of another country's progress. No tyrant in the world can conceal his cruel acts for long from the rest of mankind. A CNN reporter will be there to report on his misdoings, and it will be on the wires within 20 minutes. The killings in Tiananmen Square, so graphically illustrated on television and in still photographs, were a major setback to China's carefully crafted programme for full readmission to Western society. Who will forget the picture of the single Chinese student standing defiantly in front of a long line of Chinese tanks?

Wars and revolutions will never be the same after the media coverage of the Gulf War and the failed Soviet coup against Mikhail Gorbachev. The three CNN reporters reporting live from under their hotel beds in Baghdad on America's first strike on Iraq, the televised scenes of Moscow's ordinary citizens thronging Red Square to thwart any move by the Soviet army against Boris Yeltsin – these images and impressions linger on. No wonder that Ted Turner of CNN was made *Time* magazine's Man of the Year in 1991.

One of the implications of these advances in the organisation of the mass media is that the "rich old millions" are going to be continually bombarded with scenes of extreme wretchedness among the "poor young billions" if the world lurches down the "Low Road". The reaction of the rich is difficult to predict. Perhaps their consciences will be pricked to the extent that they will wish to reverse the situation – either directly or by applying pressure on their governments to make a positive intervention. Perhaps their senses will be dulled by the endless repetition of misery and, like the aristocrats on the terraces of Versailles Palace, they will ignore the turmoil. Or perhaps the images will terrify them to the extent that they will elect those politicians who offer extra security measures against a possible invasion by the poor: like residents of medieval castles, the rich will demand higher walls, wider moats and larger cauldrons of boiling oil to pour on all who try to scale the walls. Alas, that is the natural human reaction since security is first in Maslow's hierarchy of needs.

The "poor young billions", on the other hand, where they have access to television, are going to see endless images of the modern comforts of Triad society, forcing them constantly to make invidious comparisons with their own material circumstances. Again their response is difficult to gauge. Maybe they'll choose the recent East European and Russian option of venting their anger on their own rulers and kicking them out. Maybe they'll go the pre-World War II German route and allow themselves to be bewitched by some crazed demagogue into seeking redress for their grievances by embarking on a fullscale (and obviously futile) war against the Triad. Or maybe, as in some Islamic countries, the "poor young billions" will merely have their determination to live their lives according to a strict religious code reinforced by what they perceive as decadent images from the West.

Whichever way it goes, the relationship between the rich and the poor is going to be shaped and incessantly commented upon by the new, global media networks.

Today the most powerful "one world" symbols produced by satellite television relate to sport and entertainment. Billions tune in to the Olympic Games, soccer's World Cup, boxing's heavyweight championship of the world and pop concerts in aid of charity. They are the megaspectacles.

Our smart Roman would not have believed that audiences thousands of times larger than his circus audiences would sit glued to little boxes around the world watching the same event – seeing the same blades of grass on the floor of the arena and the same sweat on the brows of contestants. For me, the most uplifting experience produced by television was seeing the first pictures of the Earth from space. In those days of the Cold War, the one tenuous link between the two "superpowers" was the outstanding courage of the early American and Soviet astronauts.

## *Immigration*

Immigration is set to become the thorniest issue of the 1990s in America and Europe. In the US, the more open relationship developing with Mexico is likely to increase the flow of immigrants, legal and illegal, into states such as California. The US accepted more immigrants in the 1980s than in any previous decade. If one doubles the number of officially recorded immigrants to take account of illegal ones, it is estimated that immigration boosts the American population growth rate by 0,2 per cent per annum. That is around a quarter of the overall population increase.

Such levels of immigration will eventually alter the composition of US society in a significant way. By 2025 Spanish-speaking people will form the largest minority in America. Indeed, the word "minority" will by then be inappropriate as American society will have evolved to a position where it will be genuinely multiracial and multicultural. California – the world's seventh largest economy – is almost there now, as over a quarter of its population is Hispanic. It also has sizeable African American and Asian American communities. Nearly 60 per cent of the babies born in California in 1992 will be African American, Asian American or Latin American. Perhaps

---

**THE TIDES OF INTERNATIONAL IMMIGRATION**

* **Strains showing in US society, particularly in the states along the 2 000-mile Mexican border**
* **Europeans schizophrenic towards immigrants from Eastern Europe and ex-Soviet Union**
* **Japan will exclude all but highly skilled foreigners**
* **Migration everywhere will increase**

---

*Chart 14*

it's the recession in the "sunshine state" or specifically the decline of the defence industry there, but California's hardening attitude towards immigration does not bode well for the rest of America. Californians are complaining that their existing tax burden is onerous and that each new immigrant family requires additional educational, health and frequently welfare facilities. How much, who pays and when, are the questions now being asked in a spirit very different from the openhearted generosity that welcomed young immigrants in the 1950s and 1960s.

Hard and soft liberals in the United States converge in their attitudes towards immigration: hard liberals believe that immigrants help keep the labour market flexible, soft liberals value the cultural diversity that immigrants bring. Both underplay the social strains that creep into society as it becomes more disparate, strains which could conceivably erode the sense of national purpose as well as national community. The "melting pot" theory which held that the Great American Dream would mould people into true Americans looks distinctly ragged around the edges. For a start, people are arguing about what constitutes a "true American". Should he or she be like you or me? Should children be taught to become European, African, Spanish or Asian Americans – or a little bit of each? The problem is that most ordinary people grow up with one language, one culture, one history predominating in their lives, with perhaps a smattering of knowledge about the others. The strongest social forces in their lives are their family, school and immediate neighbourhood – not society at large. And when these schools and neighbourhoods are, for the most part, monocultural – a mosaic of separate Italian, Chinese, African, Korean, Latin, Old-Protestant-European communities – the American glue begins to come unstuck. Overlaying new waves of immigrants on a society which is already fragmenting only serves to deepen the divisions. Each immigrant is pigeonholed into his or her clan rather than absorbed into the wider community.

Nothing illustrates this tension better than the controversy surrounding the "Politically Correct" movement on US university campuses. This advocates that courses and faculties should reflect the new, multicultural state of US society. The opposition insists that universities are centres of excellence so professors and books should be selected entirely on merit – irrespective of cultural background. Naturally the main battleground is not objective subjects like science and mathematics where the principle of "one truth" applies, but the more subjective ones like history and literature where angles of perception count. The "Politically Correct" movement argues that in these fields any fact or standard of excellence is relative and therefore all perspectives must be articulated to the students. For example, take Christopher Columbus – does one celebrate the 500th anniversary of his discovery of America or not? Was he an intrepid explorer bringing Western civilisation to the New World or a mass murderer of indigenous people? Does one describe King Ferdinand and Queen Isabella who sent him as forward-looking monarchs for financing his voyage, or as dreadful anti-Semitic despots for banishing more than 100 000 Jews from Spain at the same time? Multiculturalism certainly makes life more interesting!

For all the apprehensions expressed, American society is infinitely adaptable. It may well find in the long run innovative ways of reinspiring sufficiently broad loyalties to overarch the clannish divisions. After all, the United States is still united. Ultimately the "American way" rubs off on any new immigrant: the esprit de corps of belonging to the greatest nation on Earth is very catching. Perhaps the fire under the "melting pot" merely needs rekindling so that the ingredients which have started to separate out come together again. The most effective way of doing this is a reasonable standard of living for everybody.

On the other side of the Atlantic Ocean, Europe is more brittle, more old-fashioned, more ill-prepared and quite schizophrenic about immigration. Europeans sympathise, but they don't want to be inundated. On a recent visit to Austria I noticed that the windows of many houses in Vienna were barred. I asked an Austrian in a tavern: "Why are you barring the windows of your houses?" He said: "We're desperately worried about poverty-stricken Eastern Europeans descending on us. We really are in the front line."

The typical Italian reaction to boatloads of Albanians trying to enter Italy through its eastern ports was: where is this going to happen next? Right-wing parties throughout Europe are garnering a greater percentage of the local, regional and national polls with anti-immigration platforms. Centre parties, sensing the drift in national consciousness, are taking a tougher line on refugees and would-be immigrants. In Germany the far right "skinheads" have mounted a series of vicious attacks on foreigners. It would seem that Western Europe is veering towards the medieval option of improving the fortification of its castles. Thus it hopes to withstand invasions from the "poor young billions" from the east and south in the event of civil wars (like that raging in Bosnia-Hercegovina) or prolonged economic misery there.

The third member of the Triad, Japan, will continue as a minor participant in immigration flows. As a group of islands it is unlikely to come under great pressure to let people in. Nevertheless the Bank of Japan has recently called for a review of the very strict limits on migrant workers, citing concerns that a growing scarcity of labour, particularly in younger age groups, might impinge negatively on the economy in the late 1990s.

Australia, which has long been well respected for its positive attitude to immigration, is taking a harder line because of domestic unemployment. The permissible total has been reduced from 111 000 to 80 000 migrants a year. Elsewhere in the world, with far less visibility, refugees flee to other lands by foot, by boat, by any means to escape the unspeakable cruelty of tyranny or the terrible ravages of civil war. They eke out a hopeless existence in temporary accommodation. For example, nearly 56 000 Vietnamese "boat people" have been living in Hong Kong but they are soon to be repatriated. In the short term, migration everywhere is set to increase despite attempts to restrict it. The economic differentials between developed and developing countries will widen before they (possibly) narrow. Travel is cheaper, immigration costs less and substantial existing immigrant communities in the Triad often facilitate the movement and accommodation of new immigrants. Borders are porous and the arrangement of illegal immigration is a growth business. As one "poor young billion" affirmed: "The straightest line between my present condition and being part of the developed world is to get there as soon as possible."

*The Spread of Aids*

Finally there is Aids. Aids, sadly, affects every country. It is now almost a decade since the beginning of a global epidemic was first recognised (the virus was identified in 1983). Many aspects such as the probability of viral transmission, pathogenesis (how HIV causes Aids), the role of cofactors and the duration of the disease from HIV infection to death are at best poorly understood. All figures quoted about the current situation have to be treated with extreme caution on the ground that the collection of data from developing countries is sometimes highly questionable. Projections are even more hazardous. Nevertheless the World Health Organisation (WHO) estimates that by early 1992 between 9 million and 11 million adults and a million children were infected by the virus worldwide. They suspect that to date perhaps 1,5 million adults and 500 000 children have developed or died of full-blown Aids (the reported figure is much lower).

WHO estimates that by the year 2000 the cumulative number of seropositive cases will have risen to 30 million adults and 10 million children. The cumulative figure for full-blown Aids victims could be 10 million by then, a large proportion of whom will have died during

---

**HIV AND AIDS**

* ✳ HIV virus identified in 1983 – still many uncertainties
* ✳ In 1992 approximately 9 to 11 million adults and one million children HIV+ in world. Cumulative Aids cases 2 million of which many have died
* ✳ By 2000 some 30 million adults and 10 million children could be HIV+ – one half of one year's global population growth
* ✳ Africa worst hit with some urban populations 15 to 20 per cent HIV+
* ✳ Asia the next vulnerable area
* ✳ Education vital as no vaccine will be available until at least turn of century

---

*Chart 15*

# PREVALENCE OF HIV IN AFRICA
## Percentage of "general" sexually active population infected with HIV-1*

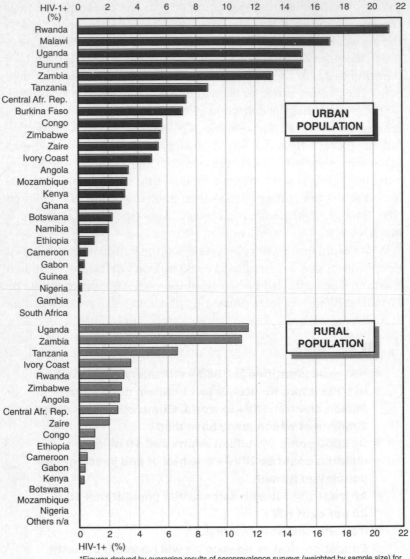

\*Figures derived by averaging results of seroprevalence surveys (weighted by sample size) for each country over the period 1985 - 89

SOURCE: Dr Paul Missen, Research and Economic Services Department, London

*Chart 16*

50

the present decade. Around 90 per cent of all seropositive and full-blown Aids cases will occur in developing countries, whose health care systems are worst equipped to cope. Tuberculosis is now recognised as one of the most common opportunistic infections to afflict Aids patients (it is found in one-third). The treatment of TB is therefore likely to become a major component of the overall cost of Aids care.

Undoubtedly, 40 million seropositive cases at the end of the century (unofficial estimates are much higher) represent a terrible number of people and a terrible amount of human tragedy. But it is one half of one year's global population growth. In other words, Aids is not yet like the Black Death which devastated Europe's population in the mid-14th Century. It will lower population growth, but it will not cause an absolute reduction in the world's numbers over the next 10 years.

This is not to say that certain countries and continents will not be very badly hit. Africa is at the forefront. About 60 per cent of infected adults so far have been in Africa compared to 10 per cent each in Latin America/the Caribbean and North America, and 5 per cent in Western Europe. Moreover, the transmission of the infection from mother to baby is common in Africa. The seroprevalence level in the sexually active urban population is probably between 15 and 20 per cent in the worst affected African countries including Rwanda, Malawi, Uganda and Burundi. It is judged that seroprevalence in urban populations is considerably higher than in rural areas. In "high risk" categories which include patients with sexually transmitted diseases, prisoners and military personnel, seroprevalence is thought to rise to over 50 per cent. The time taken for seroprevalence to double during the initial stages of the epidemic has been estimated to range from one to three years in high-prevalence African countries to five or more years in countries where prevalence is low. The window of opportunity for taking action to keep seroprevalence low is very short when you consider that any educational programme has to reach a large proportion of the population and then change their ingrained habits. It's a sobering thought that the time lag between countries at the lowest point of seroprevalence and the ones at the top end is nine years if the disease is allowed freely to

# TRENDS IN HIV-1 SEROPREVALENCE, 1985-90
## Proportion of urban pregnant women infected with HIV-1

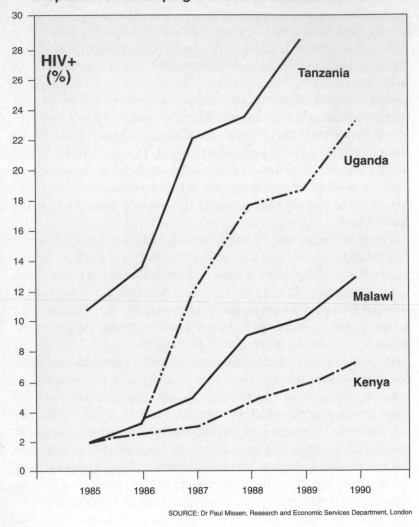

SOURCE: Dr Paul Missen, Research and Economic Services Department, London

*Chart 17*

proceed. Nonetheless, the doubling time for seroprevalence will eventually increase, as is the case with any epidemic, as the number of uninfected individuals who are "at risk" gradually diminishes.

Although it is expected to take many decades for population growth in any African country to fall to zero owing to Aids (even the ones whose towns have reached a 20 per cent seroprevalence level), the socio-economic impact of the disease will be devastating long before that moment is reached. Aids will shortly become the leading cause of death in both infants and adults: it is claimed that this is already the case in the West African city of Abidjan (and among men aged between 25 and 34 in Caribbean countries and the United States). Premature deaths will reduce the supply of skilled and unskilled labour. Within the workforce itself, absenteeism and sick leave will soar and productivity will decline. Hospitals and hospices will be overloaded as many Aids patients are incapacitated long before their death. Worst of all, one can see precursors of a plague mentality developing towards Africa. It's nothing serious as yet: but it would be an absolute tragedy if caution turned to prejudice and the Triad shunned Africa when Africa needed the Triad most.

Elsewhere in the world, India and Thailand are considered vulnerable to the rapid spread of Aids during the 1990s. In both countries seroprevalence among "high risk" groups has already risen steeply. WHO suggests that in the second half of this decade more Asians in South and Southeast Asia will be infected annually than Africans.

To combat Aids a three-pronged attack is being mounted throughout the world: education, a search for a vaccine, and a search for a cure. Education to promote abstinence, monogamy and safe sex appears to have been successful in Western countries. The number of new HIV infections each year peaked in "high risk" groups in the United States in the mid-1980s. Whether it will increase again as a result of Aids spreading to the general population is as yet unclear. In developing countries the educational task is much harder because Aids is an invisible disease and takes so long to affect the victim physically. The nightmare is that by the time Aids is killing so many people that a clear warning exists, seroprevalence will have reached a level that makes the disease unstoppable. This should not deter widespread campaigns in every country starting with schoolchildren aged between nine and 11. Changes in behaviour, particularly in the pattern of mixing between "low risk" and "high risk" groups, can

# LIFE CYCLE OF HIV IN THE HUMAN CELL
# AND POTENTIAL TARGETS OF DRUG THERAPY

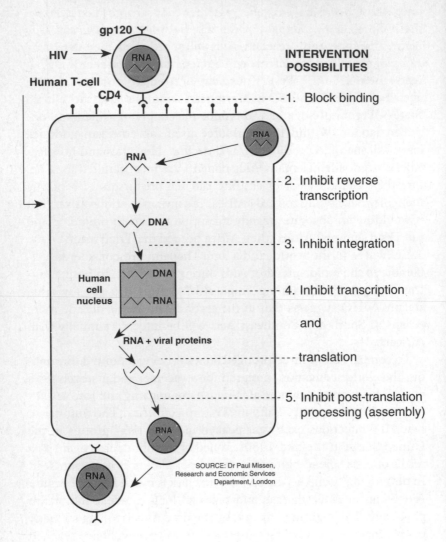

*Chart 18*

54

have a disproportionately significant impact in countries where the incidence of infection is low to moderate at present.

There are various intervention possibilities to stop the replication process of the HIV virus. No cure or vaccine exists at the moment but a large number of drugs are being tested. The two drugs currently available are AZT and ddI which have both been designed to inhibit reverse transcription and thereby extend patients' lives. The concept of combination therapy, using a cocktail of drugs to slow the disease and fight opportunistic infections, is gaining popularity. In countries able to afford a variety of treatments it may not be long before HIV infection becomes part of the growing class of chronic diseases. However, for most developing countries the cost of using combinations of therapeutic drugs will remain prohibitive. What is required is an efficient and cheap vaccine. Not until the mid-1990s will provisional results be available on various vaccines under study and not till the end of the century will definitive conclusions be reached. Even then a vaccine may offer protection against only a limited range of the various strains of HIV, not all of them. Moreover, there is evidence of a new Aids virus which may not even be HIV. Be that as it may, an earlier breakthrough cannot be ruled out, given the number of world-class research teams working on a vaccine or a cure.

## Technology

Let's move to the second "rule of the game" – technology. Every generation has its life transformed by a particular technology. If you go back to the beginning of the 19th Century, it was the railways which opened up Britain and America. In the late 19th Century it was electricity that changed the lives of Victorians: no more messy, flickering oil lamps. At the beginning of this century it was the motor car which made transport more flexible for Edwardians and created the suburbs (and now "exurbs" farther out) around cities. In the 1930s it was television, which stopped family conversation and reading for ever. The average American child now has a diet of 11 hours of television a week and 11 minutes of conversation with

**TECHNOLOGY**

* Lives of each generation transformed by particular invention, e.g. steam engine, electricity, car, TV and jet propulsion
* Current wave is Microelectronics:
  Dispersing labour into smaller units because of automation
  Individualising consumption by smarter production lines
* Next wave is Biotechnology:
  New plants, animals, trees and drugs
* Reduction in cost of communication and transport
* Rejuvenating smoke-stack industries
* Conserving base metals and energy
* Rescuing the environment

*Chart 19*

his or her father. No marks for guessing which wins in terms of influence at a very sensitive age. Family dynamics has been turned upside down by the little box in the living room. One arresting statistic is that 60 per cent of American families did not purchase a book last year. This may be due to an ultra-efficient library network, but I have a feeling that in many households the video has replaced the book as a source of entertainment. One educationist asked: "Can we ABC while we MTV?" The 1950s produced the airline jet, which made any place in the world accessible within 24 hours and turned tourism into the biggest industry in the world. What would London be without the innumerable crocodiles of different nationalities being led around Westminster Abbey by hearty, flag-waving guides?

*Microelectronics*

Now we live with microelectronics. What is microelectronics? Well, a computer the size of a room in the 1950s can now be held in the palm of your hand or strapped to your arm like a watch (a wearable personal computer with video display). At the same time the price of computing power shrank, in real terms, by a factor of 6 000. The Koreans have produced a tiny, portable video cassette recorder cum television. Formula-1 racing will never be the same now that light little electronic control units are being installed on the cars to manage the suspension and gearbox. Even more incredible, the Japanese are designing a micro-camera that can propel itself through human blood vessels. With many of these wonders go batteries that are lighter, thinner and more energy-intensive than the torchlight batteries we're used to. That's what "micro" really means.

Since 1870 the diffusion of the various technological waves has been followed by economic upswings called Kondratieff waves (named after the Russian who first drew attention to these long-term cycles). Microelectronics together with the new communication technologies has permeated a wider range of applications in products and processes than any previous technology. But the wave

## THE DIFFUSION OF TECHNOLOGICAL WAVES

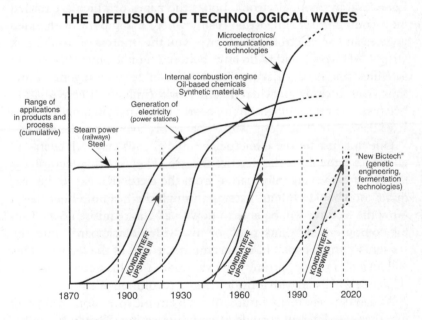

SOURCE: Adapted from Freeman, "Biotechnology, Economic and Wider Impacts", Paris, OECD (1989)

*Chart 20*

57

is nowhere near the shore yet. Advances in microelectronics are opening up a whole new series of uses. Technology to turn handwriting on a computer pad into simple text-and-graphics is already with us and voice recognition will follow as the next step. We won't have to see only Dick Tracy on film sending messages via his watch: a wearable personal computer will do it for you and function as your diary, addressbook and notepad.

Xerox has perfected a special kind of smart paper so that you can fax your personal computer to perform specific activities such as retrieving information from a file, manipulating it and sending you the answer. A sample of other products and services being designed are: videophones to talk to your friends and see their expressions or, when linked to a CAT scan, to allow a surgeon to examine a patient a thousand miles away (tele-medicine); user-friendly video cassette recorders (how many people can programme theirs?); live link-ups between your television and video libraries so you don't need to visit video shops; digital high definition televisions where the pictures are unbelievably sharp; electronic books the pages of which are turned on a computer screen; virtual reality where a computer with video goggles and an electronic glove gives you the impression you're in a virtual 3-D world; and radio links between mobile phones/faxes and satellites ringing the Earth so that you can contact anyone at any time from literally anywhere in the world (imagine a conversation between an anthropologist in the heart of the Amazon jungle and his stockbroker strolling along Wall Street to his favourite restaurant).

One final use for these microelectronic gizmos may well be in – of all places – the university lecture theatre. They say that lecturing is the art of conveying information from the lecturer's text to the students' notebooks without passing through the head of either party. Now the lecturer will be able to download the requisite notes from his computerised "think pad" or his "video-blackboard" into the students' "think pads" in an instant at the end of the lecture. This will give him the opportunity to extemporise on his notes, while the audience will listen with arms folded – a revolution in education!

As can be seen, many future microelectronic inventions will bring together the different strands of communication. They'll be multimedia: televisions aligned with personal computers, personal computers aligned with telephones and so on. Japanese and American companies are already pooling their skills and jointly developing some of the products. AT&T has teamed up with NEC to design 64-megabit chips and Texas Instruments has done a similar deal with Hitachi. Motorola and Toshiba are developing microprocessors for high definition television. Intel and Matsushita are getting together as are Advanced Micro Devices and Sony. Japan makes the boxes, America inserts the software. There's plenty of synergy to be had between the two. The latest deal involves a European company as well. Toshiba, IBM and Siemens are collaborating in a long-term venture to produce a 256-megabit chip.

How is microelectronics transforming our lives? The answer is in two fundamental ways: first, it is dispersing people into smaller and smaller units of production. Automation – in the form of the word processor, the personal computer, the robot and the numerically controlled machine tool – is eliminating the lesser-skilled white collar and blue collar jobs in big business. Concurrently the personal computer is facilitating the establishment of small businesses from scratch because it assists the entrepreneur in many of the basic functions such as planning and bookkeeping. The *Fortune 500* companies in the US have eliminated 3,5 million jobs in the last 10 years. General Motors recently announced a 74 000 cut in its workforce and IBM 20 000. Now 50 per cent of Americans work in businesses of fewer than 200 people, 30 per cent of the British in businesses of fewer than 20 people. Six out of seven Japanese work in small business, and 95 per cent of the jobs being created in the world these days are in medium-sized and small business together with the informal sector.

The second major change being wrought by microelectronics is in the field of individualising consumption. When I was recently in Tokyo I went into a Toyota showroom to see what it was like buying a new car in Japan. I went up to the salesman and said: "I'd like to buy a Toyota Lexus, please." I chose the Lexus because a British car magazine had just voted it the number one car in the world, marginally ahead of the Rolls Royce Silver Spirit. Anyway, the salesman politely ushered me to a console with a screen behind it. He pressed a button on his console and up on the screen, in computer-aided

59

3-D diagrammatic form, came a Lexus. He said: "Would you like me to spin it round for you?" I said: "Yes." He pressed the button and spun it horizontally. He then said: "Would you like to see it end-over-end?" I said: "Sure," so he complied. He asked: "Is that the exact model you want?" I responded affirmatively. He then inquired: "What colour would you like it?" so I said: "Black." He pressed another button and the car went black on the screen. He continued: "What colour would you like the upholstery to be?" so I said: "Red." So he made the upholstery red on the screen. Every accessory I wanted he put on the screen, and then he said: "Is that the car you want?" so I said: "Yes, but unfortunately I'm a tourist here so I can't buy it, but what do you usually do next?" He said: "I press this button and that information, without any human intervention whatsoever, is automatically down-loaded onto the bank of computers on the Toyota production line 100 kilometres away, and six days later your car will come out as a production run of one." The Japanese call this "flexible manufacturing". It's very different from the days in America when 14 million Model-T Fords were produced which were identically black. You have to personalise a brand these days when most goods – like cars and television sets – are basically no more than engineered commodities. A strong brand image is the only way to add real value to the product or service you are selling. This is why companies are taken over for their brands, and why brands are accorded a significant value in many balance sheets.

Another example I heard about in Tokyo concerned a large jewellery store in the Ginza district, Tokyo's equivalent of Knightsbridge in London. If you're a woman wishing to purchase a jewellery piece, the shop takes a photograph of you and puts your image on a video screen. Instead of trying jewellery on, you quickly flick a thousand pieces across your image until you find the right one. If your choice is not immediately available on the shop floor, the computer will order it up from the basement or locate it elsewhere in Tokyo. You get exactly what you desire as an individual.

So microelectronics is individualising society. It's demassifying it, changing the pattern of production and consumption. Instead of large clumps of unskilled people working on an assembly line under a single factory roof, you have small clusters of highly skilled techni-

## RELATIVE SOURCES OF COMPETITIVE ADVANTAGE

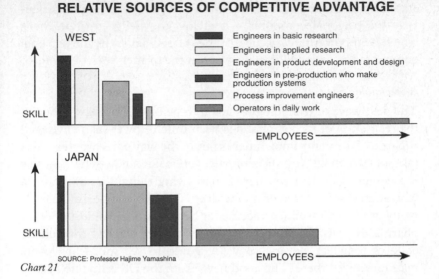

*Chart 21*

cians, maintenance engineers and operators. Witness the contrast between the labour force of a modern Japanese company and the conventional structure of a Western company. The modern Japanese company has more engineers in applied research, product development and design, production systems and process improvement than the Western company (though fewer in basic research). Hence a lot more effort goes into the front-end job of designing the product, and into simplifying the process to produce it in order to reduce lead times and cut labour to a minimum (thereby maximising value added per person). The labour force is much smaller and at the same time more highly trained in the Japanese company, so that the production line can be varied for the needs of individual customers without reducing quality. The revenue per employee of Nintendo, a Japanese home video games specialist, is $4,9 million compared to, say, $16 000 per gold miner in South Africa.

One of the first casualties of the dispersion of labour into smaller businesses is the trade union movement. Membership of British and American trade unions is at its lowest level for 30 years. Self-employed people don't unionise themselves. George Orwell got it wrong in his book *1984*. He said the computer would empower the state against the individual. What the computer is doing – particularly the personal computer – is giving knowledge to individuals which is empowering *them* against the state. That's why the personal computer was banned for many years in the former Soviet Union.

### Biotechnology

The next wave of technology is going to be biotechnology, although the realisation of its potential has been much slower than envisaged because of the many impediments put in the way of its progress. You take a DNA chain, you slice it apart, you insert a new gene, you sew it together again and you have a new living thing – a new plant, a new animal, a new tree or a new drug. Genetic engineering has already produced insulin, a vaccine for hepatitis B and a host of other pharmaceuticals. In Wales a scientist has just cracked the genetic code of four-leaf clovers, so we're going to see four-leaf clovers mass-produced there. The good news from the US is that no special approvals will be needed for the marketing of many bio-engineered fruits and vegetables. The first one likely to be available is a tomato

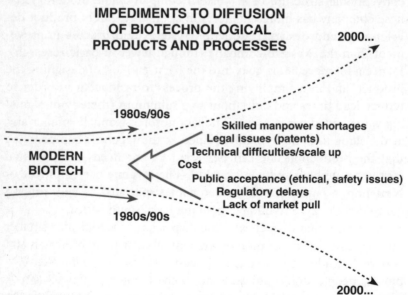

Chart 22

**IMPORTANT BIOTECH-DERIVED PHARMACEUTICALS
LAUNCHED BETWEEN 1982 AND 1989**

* ✳ INSULIN ("Humulin"): Ranked 39 in the world's 50 top-selling drugs (1990 sales, $360m)
* ✳ TPA plasminogen activator ("Activase"): 1990 sales $215m, up from $154m in its launch year (1988)
* ✳ HGH, human growth hormone ("Protropin"): Japanese sales in 1989 of $110m
* ✳ FACTOR VIII clotting agent ("Monoclate")
* ✳ HEPATITIS B VACCINE ("Recombivax") and several animal vaccines
* ✳ ALPHA-INTERFERON ("Intron"/"Referon") and GAMMA-INTERFERON
* ✳ EPO, erythropoetin ("Marogen"/"Epogen"), just outside top 50 drugs in 1990 with sales of $250m
* ✳ Around 250 diagnostic tests for humans (mostly monoclonal antibody-based, some DNA probes), sales approximately $600m, and well over 100 tests for animals
* ✳ *Genetically engineered DNA drugs and diagnostic tests represent around 2% of US pharmaceutical industry sales*

*Chart 23*

in which the gene that produces a rot-inducing enzyme has been de-activated. American scientists have also genetically engineered an enzyme which you put into cows' stomachs so that they can produce 20 per cent more milk. But, of course, more milk means less cow, so the cows are quite small and they get lost in long grass. Nevertheless, they are super-cows! Perhaps we'll have super-sheep one day that can automatically shed their fleeces. But what is really needed is bionic cattle that eat less grass and drink less water per kilogram of meat produced. The average member of the present herd chomps its way through 410 kilograms of vegetation every month. Because of the environmental damage this causes, cattle have been termed "hoofed locusts".

Biotech developments since the early 1980s are influencing many fields of human endeavour. The most exciting prospect is gene therapy. Instead of using bacteria to mass-produce proteins which are then injected into patients, scientists are taking the short cut of putting the gene that produces the desired protein straight into the patient. This could be a breakthrough for single-gene diseases like

---

**"NEW" BIOTECHNOLOGY
DEVELOPMENTS SINCE THE EARLY EIGHTIES**

NEW PRODUCTS

∗ *Pharmaceuticals:* More than 10 new drugs and vaccines. 200+ new diagnostic tests. Transgenic animals ("drug factories", disease models)
∗ *Agriculture:* Herbicide-, insect- and virus-resistant plants/crops. Genetic modification of cereals attained (and infection with nitrogen-fixing bacteria). New diagnostics and therapeutics for animals
∗ *Food:* Commercialisation of mycoprotein for human consumption
∗ *Biosensors:* A large number available

NEW TECHNOLOGIES

∗ *Protein engineering:* Improved industrial enzymes, modified drugs and monoclonal antibodies (including catalytic antibodies)
∗ *Gene therapy* in humans
∗ *Novel assays/screens* for drug selection
∗ Polymerase chain reaction (PCR): "Genetic finger printing", amplification of DNA
∗ *Ribozymes:* Potential for antiviral treatment (cf. antibodies against bacteria)

---

*Chart 24*

cystic fibrosis. At a more distant date, applying genetic engineering to the field of bioelectronics could yield "biochips" for computers. Moreover, the prospect of "designer babies" can no longer be taken with a pinch of salt.

### Other Applications

Technology is also revolutionising communication and transport. It's dramatically reducing the cost. A telephone call is now 70 times cheaper in real terms than it was in 1930. An airfare is seven times cheaper than it was in 1930. So what technology has done is to bring communication and transport to the masses.

Technology is also rejuvenating smokestack industries. The steel industry has been going through a period of major change. In the past two decades, the replacement of open hearth production with oxygen and electric arc furnaces has largely been completed in the market economy countries. The key efficiency issue now is the further development of continuous casting from the slab stage, which is the norm, to thin-slabs and ultimately thin-sheet. At the same time, environmental pressures are driving steel producers to look for technologies which will allow them to eliminate coke ovens.

Thanks to technology, there will be no shortage of base metals and energy. The Club of Rome got it wrong in 1972. They said the world would start running out of resources in the year 2000. What they didn't count on was man's ingenuity in finding substitutes when a material ran short, or in using that particular material more cleverly. For example you have optical fibre which is now replacing copper in telephone lines. The amount of copper, lead, zinc and tin used per unit of industrial production is declining at 1 to 2 per cent per annum. Nevertheless, because the rate of growth of industrial production normally exceeds the decline in intensity, absolute demand for base metals has shown a healthy increase for most of the 1980s. And the future does not look bad either. When the world economy recovers, there will be an upsurge in base metals demand to satisfy the next investment cycle in plant and machinery. The Triad one day has to renew its ageing infrastructure of roads and bridges, and developing countries have to go through a metals-intensive phase to catch up with Western ownership of such necessi-

## STEEL – REVITALISATION OF A SMOKESTACK INDUSTRY THROUGH NEW TECHNOLOGY

**EFFICIENCY**

* Computerisation
* Replacing open hearth with oxygen and electric arc furnaces
* Integrated melting/rolling
* Continuous/sequence casting (less wastage)

| Ingot | ⇒ Slabs | ⇒ Thin slabs | ⇒ Thin sheet |
|---|---|---|---|
| outdated | the "norm" | NUCOR the first | next generation |

**ENVIRONMENT (Reducing the reliance on coke)**

* Move away from integrated (iron/coke) to mini (scrap/DRI) steelworks
* Blast furnace coal injection
* Developing next generation of non-coke based iron/steelmaking technology i.e. Corex, hi-smelt

**QUALITY**

* Secondary steelmaking/ladle refining (improved quality)
* Controlled rolling (including cold rolling and heat treatment)
* Closer tolerances

**NEW PRODUCTS**

* HSLA steels (improved strength/weight ratios often eliminating heat treatments)
* Coated steels (zinc, aluminium, dual alloy and organic coatings)

---

*Chart 25*

66

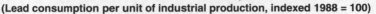

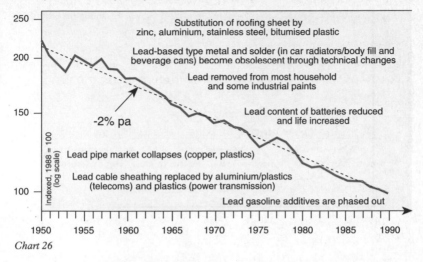

## INTENSITY OF LEAD USAGE, 1950 - 1990
### (Lead consumption per unit of industrial production, indexed 1988 = 100)

Substitution of roofing sheet by
zinc, aluminium, stainless steel, bitumised plastic

Lead-based type metal and solder (in car radiators/body fill and
beverage cans) become obsolescent through technical changes

Lead removed from most household
and some industrial paints

Lead content of batteries reduced
and life increased

-2% pa

indexed, 1988 = 100
(log scale)

Lead pipe market collapses (copper, plastics)

Lead cable sheathing replaced by aluminium/plastics
(telecoms) and plastics (power transmission)

Lead gasoline additives are phased out

*Chart 26*

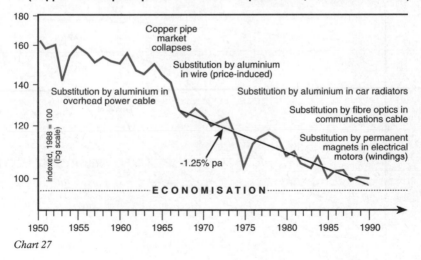

## INTENSITY OF COPPER USAGE, 1950 - 1990
### (Copper consumption per unit of industrial production, indexed 1988 = 100)

Copper pipe
market
collapses

Substitution by aluminium
in wire (price-induced)

Substitution by aluminium in car radiators

Substitution by aluminium in
overhead power cable

Substitution by fibre optics in
communications cable

indexed, 1988 = 100
(log scale)

Substitution by permanent
magnets in electrical
motors (windings)

-1.25% pa

E C O N O M I S A T I O N

*Chart 27*

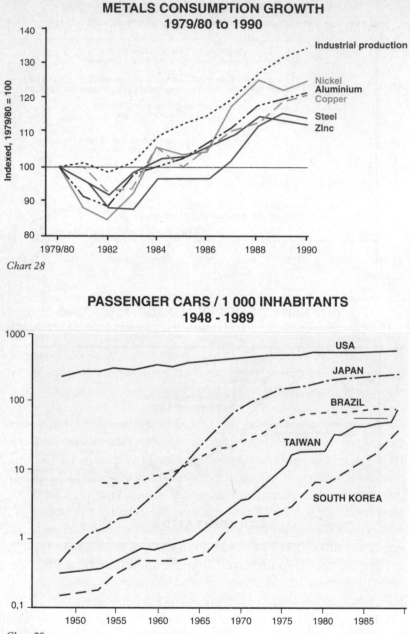

**METALS CONSUMPTION GROWTH**
**1979/80 to 1990**

*Chart 28*

**PASSENGER CARS / 1 000 INHABITANTS**
**1948 - 1989**

*Chart 29*

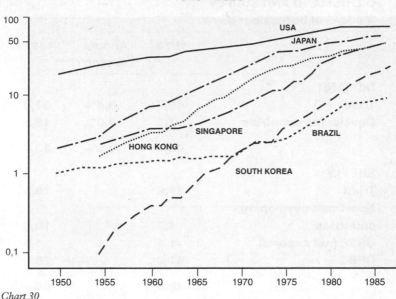

**TELEPHONES / 100 INHABITANTS**
**1948 - 1986**

*Chart 30*

ties as a car and a telephone. But the point is that there will generally be enough base metals to go around. In specific instances where there is not, substitution with a new material will take place.

The two oil price shocks have meant that around the world widespread energy conservation has occurred. Between 1973 and 1991 the call on OPEC declined from 31 million to 25 million barrels a day. The oil market is no longer under stress as current OPEC production is well below its maximum sustainable capacity of 31 million barrels a day. It is estimated that the total number of vehicles in the world will increase by 43 per cent over the next 10 years from 572 million to 820 million and yet fuel consumption will remain flat at about 22 million barrels a day of oil equivalent. It's because vehicles are getting lighter on the road. They incorporate aluminium, polymers, ceramics and composites in place of more traditional materials. Aerodynamic drag coefficients are down by 40 per cent; fourth generation radial tyres reduce rolling resistance by 10 per cent. Cars are getting leaner on petrol too. Current technology will ensure that

69

**OIL DEMAND AND SUPPLY**
**Millions of barrels per day**

| | 1973 | Annual growth | 1991 |
|---|---|---|---|
| **DEMAND** | | | |
| Triad | 40,7 | -0,4% | 37,8 |
| Developing countries | 7,8 | 4,0% | 15,5 |
| | 48,5 | 0,5% | 53,3 |
| **SUPPLY** | | | |
| Triad | 11,8 | | 16,5 |
| Non-Opec developing countries | 4,3 | | 10,5 |
| USSR (net exports) | 1,4 | | 1,3 |
| OPEC | 31,0 | | 25,0 |
| | 48,5 | | 53,3 |

**CALL ON OPEC**

| MAXIMUM SUSTAINABLE CAPACITY 1990 | | |
|---|---|---|
| 9,0 | Saudi Arabia | 7,5 |
| 3,4 | Iran | 3,2 |
| 3,5 | Iraq | |
| 2,2 | UAE | 2,3 |
| 2,4 | Kuwait | |
| 2,9 | Venezuela | 2,4 |
| 7,6 | Others | 9,6 |
| 31,0 | | 25,0 |

*Chart 31*

passenger car fuel consumption will come down from the current 8,3 to 4,6 litres per 100 km by the year 2000 – an efficiency level already available in some small cars.

The Volvo LCP 2000 with a three-cyclinder, heat-insulated, direct-injection, turbocharged engine is a step towards the ideal. A prototype has achieved 4,5 litres per 100 km with a design potential of a further 30 per cent gain in efficiency. A recent calculation showed that if all Americans drove the smaller European cars, the US would not have to import oil. That would make the tiger smile in the tank!

Lastly technology is rescuing the environment. We have the "world of science" and the "world of perception". Because scientific uncertainty still surrounds many environmental issues, the "world of perception" drives policy formulation. Global warming is a good example. For sure the chemical composition of the atmosphere is being changed by industrial gases. But as each uncertainty about these gases and what they do is followed by the next one, the result is a large pyramid of uncertainties. In particular, global climate models still have relatively simplistic treatments of cloud and ocean sys-

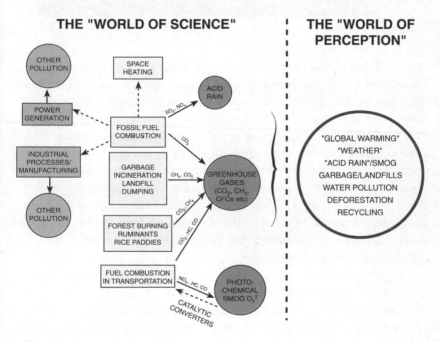

*Chart 32*

# "GLOBAL WARMING": KEY UNCERTAINTIES

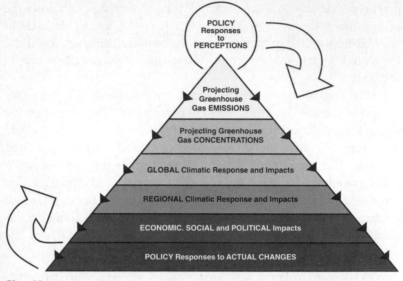

POLICY
Responses
to
PERCEPTIONS

Projecting
Greenhouse
Gas EMISSIONS

Projecting Greenhouse
Gas CONCENTRATIONS

GLOBAL Climatic Response and Impacts

REGIONAL Climatic Response and Impacts

ECONOMIC. SOCIAL and POLITICAL Impacts

POLICY Responses to ACTUAL CHANGES

*Chart 33*

tems. Thus global warming is very different from desertification, malnutrition and diarrhoea which are definitely there and which kill. But the potential downside is too great to be sensibly ignored untilthe jury is in on the link between global warming and carbon dioxide and other gases. European politicians are already mooting some form of fiscal disincentive against the burning of carbon-based fuels, such as a hybrid carbon-energy tax. Meanwhile, technologists are hunting for ways to conserve energy and reduce dependence on fossil fuels. They're coming up with better insulated homes and one company is about to market the E-Lamp, a bulb in which radio waves are cleverly converted into visible light at a fraction of the energy loss of a normal light bulb.

Another avenue being explored is improving the thermal efficiency of power stations. New conventional coal-fired stations can manage as high as 39 per cent thermal efficiency, but mechanisms to reduce sulphur dioxide and $NO_x$ (nitrogen and oxygen) emissions cut this efficiency by some 3 to 4 per cent. Efficiencies could be in-

# INTEGRATED GASIFICATION
# COMBINED CYCLE

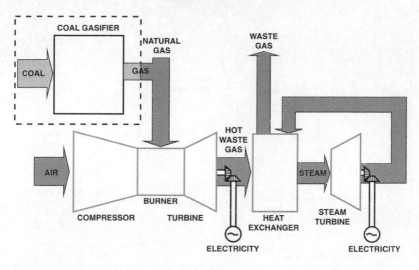

*Chart 34*

creased by integrated gasification in a combined-cycle operation. The latest power stations using gas alone are now achieving around 48 per cent thermal efficiency which in time could be pushed over 50 per cent. "Passively safe" systems of nuclear power generation, which rely on gravity and automatic systems to flood the reactor and on convection currents to carry the heat away, are being perfected too. However, the problems with nuclear power remain the high cost of meeting stringent standards and the decommissioning of obsolete plants, together with burial of waste – breaking-up is really hard to do.

Let's go back to the car again. In the Triad, transport – the car in particular – contributes three-quarters of the carbon monoxide emissions, half of the $NO_x$, 40 per cent of the hydrocarbon and around one-fifth of the carbon dioxide. In addition 125 000 Triadians are killed every year in vehicle collisions. So the car is an obvious target for environmental action. California is the pathfinder in legislating emission controls. In so doing it has precipitated sig-

# "THE CAR" – AN ARCHETYPE FOR ENVIRONMENTAL ACTION

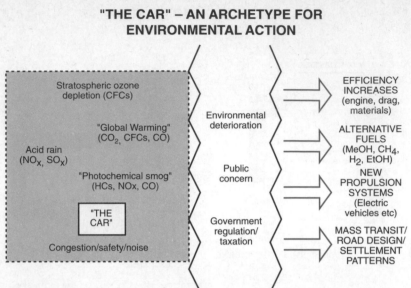

Chart 35

# THE ADVANCE OF AUTOMOTIVE EMISSION CONTROL IN THE US – A GOAL OF ZERO?

**Legislation restricting pollutant emissions and required technology**

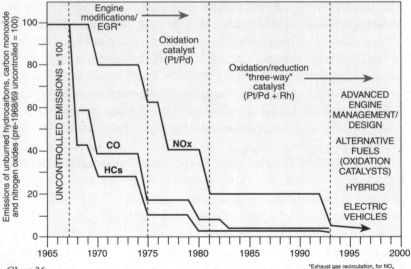

Chart 36

*Exhaust gas recirculation, for NO$_x$

nificant technology changes – notably catalytic converters. Modern cars fitted with three-way catalytic converters produce between one-fifth and one thirty-fifth (depending on the pollutants) of the emissions of unregulated cars in the 1960s. Nevertheless, because the increase in total number of cars and distances travelled has offset the savings made by reducing emissions, California has decreed that by 2003 a tenth of the new cars sold there must have "zero emission"

## ELECTRIC VEHICLE PROJECTS

| Make | Model | Volume | Production |
|------|-------|--------|------------|
| Audi | 100 Avant Quattro | 200 | Germany, 1991- |
| BMW | 320 | 10 | Germany, 1990- |
| Chrysler | Voyager | 50 | US, 1990-93 |
| Clean Air Transport | LA301 Saloon | 3500 | UK/Sweden, 1992-* |
| Fiat | Panda | 500 | Italy, 1990- |
| Ford | Aerostar ETX – II Van | 2 | US, 1989- |
| Ford | Escort | 70-100 | Europe, 1992 |
| GM | Impact Saloon | 1 | US, 1990- |
| GM | G-Van | 2500 | US, 1990- * |
| Isuzu | Elf Van | 3000 | Japan, 1994- |
| Mercedes-Benz | 190 Saloon | 6 | Germany, 1990-91 |
| Nissan | Micra Saloon | 1+ | Japan, 1989- |
| Peugeot | 205 | 30+ | France, 1990- |
| Peugeot | J5 Van | 25+ | France, 1990- |
| Peugeot | Citroen C-15 Van | 50+ | France, 1991- |
| Peugeot | 205 | – | France, 1991- |
| Toyota | Town Ace Van | 3+ | Japan, 1990- |
| Unique Mobility | Estate/Dodge Caravan | – | US, 1991-* |
| Volkswagen | Jetta | 120+ | Germany, 1991- |

*Taking part in California's "Electric Vehicle Initiative"

Source: *Financial Times*, London, 11 April 1991, Research and Economic Services Department, London

*Chart 37*

and 15 per cent ultra-low emission. At the moment only electric propulsion is capable of meeting the zero limit and providing a practical means of transport, though solar-powered and hydrogen-fuelled vehicles are potential candidates but much less developed. Ultra-low emission vehicles will be hybrids: probably electric/diesel injection with PGM-based catalysts (PGM: platinum group metals).

California's edict has spawned an immense number of projects by major car companies. None can afford to be left behind in the race for the "high performance" electric car. Of course the batteries providing power to the car must be recharged using environmentally benign electricity.

Technology will rise to the occasion – even to the extent of making the electric car completely recyclable!

### The Next 1 000 Years

In the longer term, say in the next millennium, where will technology lead us? Let's wind the clock back 2 000 years and ask the smart Roman again. He would have surveyed his villa and possibly envisaged better-insulated accommodation with improved plumbing. With cavities in his teeth he would certainly have wished for advances in dentistry. He might also have dreamed of a much faster chariot. But what he wouldn't have envisaged is the breakthrough in new materials (metals, rubber, plastics) and in new forms of energy (internal combustion, electricity) which has given us the modern motor car. Leonardo da Vinci sketched a primitive plane, but he could not have pencilled in the jet engines. As late as the mid-19th Century, studies into the congestion of horse-drawn carriages in London were published, proving that the city was shortly to sink under layers of horse manure. Nobody predicted that a new form of personal transportation was in the offing, with its own photochemical smog.

Broadly, technology over the last 2 000 years has provided us with better medical care, the ability to travel swifter and further not only on Earth but in space as well, a wider choice of clothes and foods, improved accommodation and various forms of entertainment. It has vastly increased our store of knowledge. It has also expanded our capacity to communicate and calculate. It has allowed us to fulfil our basic needs better: it has widened our options of living. So in projecting forward, why not more of the same but this time directed at improving the quality of life of the "poor young billions"? The greatest challenge is to design affordable technologies to get the rest of the world up to speed with the Triad without ruining the environment.

The way a city will look in 1 000 years' time? What our knowledge of the universe will be? I would never hazard a guess.

## Social Values

The third "rule of the game" concerns the way people think. Values change society. However, there are two ways in which people have not changed.

### Bloodlust and Roots

The first, unfortunately, is bloodlust – the desire to kill. What has happened is that weapons have become far more effective than they

---

**SOCIAL VALUES**

* **No change in:**
  **Desire to kill**
  **Desire for roots**
* **But "Second Reformation" over last five years in which ideologies have been rejected in favour of systems that work**
* **Hence collapse of Marxism**
* **Focus on economic growth being replaced by more balanced perspective involving economic development, environmental health and quality of life**

---

*Chart 38*

were in the olden days. Back in the Stone Age, if your colleague came too close to your pile of meat you bashed him on the head with a club; later you shot him with a bow and arrow, pierced him with a sword and scalped him with a tomahawk. But the tomahawk has become the Tomahawk Cruise Missile. With a nuclear warhead one weapon can kill a million people. It means that we are moving into a very dangerous period of the world's history. On the one hand we do not have a lowering in the desire to kill, but on the other hand we have an increase in the effectiveness of weapons. A lot of out-of-work Russian rocket scientists are circulating the globe at present looking for other jobs. America is putting money into Russian academies to try to keep these scientists at home. But it only needs one or two to escape the net and, for a modest fee, divulge the secrets of nuclear missile technology to one of the more dangerous rulers in the world, and geopolitics will change overnight. Knowledge is indestructible: cities are not.

Hollywood is glamorising violence. The average American teenager of 18 has witnessed 40 000 murders on television. In real life, so to speak, US society experiences 23 000 murders per year. There are 200 million firearms in private hands in the US, of which 60 million to 70 million are handguns. The second commonest cause of death among high school children involves a firearm. Arms control and gun control are equally important – arms control to stop some tinpot dictator holding the world to ransom with a nuclear device, and gun control to stop the internal disintegration of society through crime. In 1990 there were more than 12 million females living in the United States who had been raped at least once. Around 60 per cent of the rape victims were younger than 18 and 30 per cent under 11. As Martin Luther King once said: "The choice today is not between violence and non-violence. It is either non-violence or non-existence."

The second way values haven't changed is related to the desire for roots: clannishness, language, culture and religion are very strong life forces because they assist in giving an individual his or her identity.

Indeed, remembering that many nation-states are a relatively recent phenomenon formed for the purposes of attack or defence in war, one now sees the world breaking down into clans again (a cartographer's nightmare). External conditions have changed to weaken the justification for clans getting together into larger entities. Many Scots want to sever connections with England so that their country can be represented as a separate body in the European Community. A large number of French-speaking Canadians want more autonomy for Quebec. The Walloons and Flemish in Belgium are on uneasy terms. The Czechs and Slovaks are heading for a divorce after a 74-year marriage. The Basques and Catalans desire special status in Spain. The Kurds want their own state carved out of Iraq and Turkey. The Green Line continues to separate Turks and Greeks in Cyprus. And then there are the wars: Armenians versus Azeris in the former Soviet Union; Serbs versus Croats versus Muslims in Bosnia-Hercegovina. A Somali proverb sums it up: "I and Somalia against the world. I and my clan against Somalia. I and my family against the clan. I and my brother against the family. I against my brother." In much of the Third World, nation-states are artificial constructions of a bygone political era: the clans and the families are the basic bedrock. Nevertheless, one can turn the Somali proverb on its head by saying that, in favourable circumstances, an individual will have a whole array of loyalties which will dilute clan and family instincts.

Specifically, in order to overcome these life forces you have to create clubs that are worth belonging to. Take the European Community. Another war is very unlikely between Germany, France and Britain because all three belong to a worthwhile club. There are clear economic advantages to a Common Market. Moreover, the rules of the club have injected a measure of discipline into the members' lives through currency stabilisation and, looking ahead, tax equalisation. In a different dimension, each nation by broadening its contacts within the club enriches its own roots and culture. The only motive for breaking it up will be that the club becomes too expensive in terms of membership dues or the club committee tries to interfere too much in the lives of the members. Neither of these risks can be entirely discounted. On the one hand the club's dues which include farming subsidies are running at $87 billion per annum (not much less than South Africa's Gross National Product of $100 billion). On the other hand the club committee is in danger of being turned from a vehicle to further free trade into one which "Euro-Effendis" use to impose their own brand of bureaucracy on everyone else. Another potential hazard is that Euro-Effendis will continue to underestimate the nationalistic tendencies that lie deep inside each European nation. The Danish referendum of June 1992 is a warning that federalism must not be pushed too hard. If the Common Market superstructure intrudes too much on national sovereignty, the whole Maastricht accord will fall apart.

Another valued club is the United Nations for the obvious reason of global security. By contrast the Soviet Union was clearly a club not worth belonging to. No financial benefits were to be had for the members. Moreover, at one time the chairman physically restrained you if you tried to leave club premises or had you shot if you complained. It was a compulsory co-operative which was bound to dissolve when the muscle at the centre atrophied. Yugoslavia has ceased to exist for the same reason whereas 700-year-old Switzerland continues because it's worth while. Whether you're talking about a community, commonwealth, confederation, federation or even a nation-state, the principle remains that a co-operative will hold together only if it is voluntary and successful. A strong case can therefore be made for bills of rights and sometimes rights of exit in any constitution binding members to form a political co-operative of the kinds enumerated above. Otherwise minorities can cause a lot of pain in their demands for protection or self-rule, as countries have found out all over the world. It will be interesting to see whether China can withstand the worldwide trend towards decentralisation of power or, whether like the Soviet Union, it breaks down into a mosaic of new and smaller nations. There is even a lobby in the United States calling for a return to the original Articles of Confederation which served as the Constitution from 1781 to 1788!

### The Second Reformation

But there has been one crucial change over the last five years which, as I said earlier on, has been dubbed the "Second Reformation". In the first one Martin Luther nailed a set of requests to a church door which changed religion for ever. Moreover, the independence of thought he promoted was indirectly responsible for the birth of modern science and underlay much of the work of Adam Smith. The Second Reformation is shaking the political world. It's the general movement away from political ideology towards systems that work: from collectivist/welfarist assumptions towards attitudes and policies favourable to effort, risk/reward and market solutions.

The best examples come from the old Soviet Union. As usual they come in the form of humorous anecdotes. One was a cartoon in *Izvestiya* that I saw several years ago. It was of a Russian who went all the way to Moscow to see the best ear, nose and throat specialist in the country. The doctor says to him: "Comrade, you've come such a long way: you must have a very special complaint." The patient says: "I do; I cannot see what I hear." He'd heard all about *perestroika* and *glasnost*, but he went to the shops and he couldn't see it; he saw the same old shortages and the same old queues. Another is the story of the Russian waiting for two hours in a food queue. Finally he makes it to the front just when the shelves are empty. "What," he says, "no meat left?" The man behind the counter replies: "You've come to the wrong shop. This one has no bread left. It's the shop next door that has no meat left." One piece of Soviet graffiti also comes to mind: "The best place to be when the world comes to an end is the Soviet Union because it is 50 years behind the rest of the world." The writer was not aware that the Soviet Union would come to an end first simply because it didn't work.

So, as I was saying, we're moving into a much more pragmatic period of the world's history. People are no longer being duped by single ideas, by ideologies peddled by ideologues. They are looking for something more sophisticated. What most people believe is that life is now a complex system of trade-offs, a mixture of opposites. Heavy trends in values are slow to evolve and slow to dissipate. There was evidence as early as the end of the 1960s of a movement towards liberty and individualism, away from equality and collectivisation. The closest one can come to the new "complexity paradigm" is ironically the ancient Chinese philosophy of the yin and the yang: the yin of light, the yang of darkness; the yin of good, the yang of evil. Generosity, selfishness; justice, mercy; competition, co-operation; truth, falsehood: the list of opposites is endless. In other words, life is a

**HEAVY TRENDS IN THE 1990s (WESTERN EUROPE)**

1 *Autonomy:* Individual freedom, self-determination; a challenge to institutions of all types
2 *Vitality:* Inhibitions to sensual/emotional experiences have been declining for several decades
3 *Organic social fabric:* A move from fragmentation to integration/completeness
4 *Systems:* Reality as understood through the concept of interconnectedness
5 *Need for authentic meaning:* A move from tradition and ideology to fulfilment through individual experiences

*Chart 39*

duality of qualities and anti-qualities. Why? Because one quality brings out the other and duality gives us choice. Republican or Democrat, Tory or Labour, capitalism or socialism – what would one be without the other? Even modern physics has succumbed to this philosophy with its description of an electron as a particle and a wavicle and its discovery that both matter and anti-matter exist. So single ideas just don't capture the richness of the world.

In the shift in values in Western Europe, the duality is expressed in the move to more individual freedom and autonomy on the one hand but the growing realisation of the interconnectedness and integration of the world on the other (the "holism" of Jan Smuts, the "Gaia" of James Lovelock). Let's expand on the latter concept. If you chop down a tree the sum of the parts, the dead logs, is not the same as the original living tree. The laws of mathematical addition do not apply to living or social organisms. Why? Because the relationships between members of living or social organisms matter as much as the intrinsic worth of each member considered by itself. One season a football team wins the league, the next it comes bottom, with the same individuals. The magic between the players is there one year, gone the next. Marriage/divorce, corporate success/

82

failure, environmental health/degradation all depend on the presence or absence of social harmony. It is ironic that exactly when people the world over are converting to the rigorous individualism of free enterprise, the necessity for collective action is growing in order to save the planet.

The bad Effendis have no understanding of social organisms. They feel that such organisms can be altered by decree, or better still by social engineering. They do not believe in the natural, organic development of societies. Moreover, they are oblivious to the subtle interplay in human emotions where response and counter-response have to be weighed up very carefully before a particular course of action is pursued. As the former Soviet Union has demonstrated, too overt an urge to be centripetal elicits a centrifugal response. Power really is paradoxical. The more you try to seize it, the more it turns into an illusion. Conversely, the lighter the bonds, the more tightly they bind.

### A Balanced Approach

Life is ultimately a balance between three competing priorities: economic development for the clothes you wear, the food you eat, the house you live in and the job you have; environmental health for clean air, clean beaches, clean rivers, fertile land, and to pass on a heritage to your children; and quality of life, which is quite apart from the physical universe. People need spiritual fulfilment and a sense of idealism (as opposed to ideology). They want autonomy and independence, family and friends, health and vitality and the satisfaction of a job well done. Their lives are incomplete without tradition and stimulation; hence the necessity for old buildings to be preserved in places like Italy where there are serious signs of decay and for a thriving arts industry to be cultivated in every country. Voltaire warned a long time ago: "In one half of our life we sacrifice our health in order to earn money, in the other we sacrifice money to regain our health. And while we are doing so, health and life pass us by." If you introspect a little on your motivations for doing things, there is as much happiness to be had out of actions to help others as there is out of actions to help yourself. Money isn't everything. A society without charity is as deficient as one without free enterprise.

## THE THREE DETERMINANTS OF
## HUMAN WELLBEING

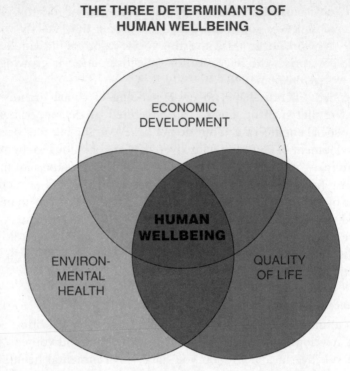

*Chart 40*

A poignant story highlighting the importance of balance was given to me by Ken Tinley, an environmentalist. It concerns the introduction of Cheviot sheep into Scotland in the late 18th and early 19th Centuries. The sheep, a new breed at the time and hardy enough to withstand the rigours of the Scottish climate, displaced crofters who had been on the moors and mountains for centuries. The economic arguments were obvious. The Scottish lairds made 12 times as much out of the sheep per acre as the rent they charged the crofters. But the long-term social consequences for Scotland of the "Highland clearances" were drastic. After much instability in the first half of the 19th Century, the homeless crofters emigrated to other lands. Scotland's loss was the world's gain.

What one constantly has to do is try to juggle the three priorities mentioned above against one another. Too great an obsession with economic development ruins the environment and quality of life, as many of the newly industrialising economies have found to their cost. In Bangkok, for instance, the average commuter stares at the rear bumper of the vehicle in front for 42 days a year. Closer to home, one young Durban surfer put it like this: "What's the use of the latest surfboard technology if you're baking to death because there's no ozone left?"

On the other hand, if you think only about eating berries and riding bicycles you create unemployment queues. Hence the motivation of the ecological movement is changing. Germany is setting the pace in making the preservation of the environment a natural extension of the economy. To bring an end to the throwaway society, stringent new rules have been enacted to make the actual sources of any paper, plastic, metal or other packaging responsible for its recycling or its disposal. Manufacturers and retailers will have to plan more carefully how they are going to cover their products and the type of materials to be used, in order to minimise the on-cost to the customer. The principle of "user pays" will, I'm sure, be used in many other fields where a "social cost" to the environment is incurred.

The US is harnessing the drive of the free market in a different way to limit pollution. The 1990 Clean Air Act imposes a ceiling on

---

**ENVIRONMENTAL ATTITUDES**

**The ecological movement**
* **not declining but deeply changing from**
   *ideological* **(opposition of "capitalist" technology) and**
* *emotional* **(nostalgia)**
   **to** *rational*,
   **egoistic not altruistic,**
   **acceptance of technology**
   **acceptance of complexity and uncertainty**

---

*Chart 41*

the amount of pollution allowed in a given area of a particular kind. Those enterprises that reduce their emissions more than their share requires can sell their surplus to companies that find it inordinately expensive to meet the limit. These "emission rights" can be freely traded provided the aggregate remains below the permitted emission level for the region. This flexibility allows the market to determine the most efficient way (in terms of least cost) to meet the environmental targets set. The first deal of this nature has recently been

---

**VALUES IN THE UNITED STATES IN THE 1990s**

**VALUES ON THE UPSWING**
* **Neo-traditionalism**
  **"Sobering" of the psychological and consumer environments**
* **Neo-conservatism**
* **Neo-conservationism**
* **Family values**
  **Greater focus on marital longevity. Protectionism towards the family**
* **Search for meaning and substance**
* **Individualism and choice of priorities**
* **Setting limits**
* **Health and quality of life**

*Represents a search for balance*
*Intangible goals are starting to replace the acquisition of tangibles*

**VALUES ON THE DOWNSWING**
* **Entitlement (to consume)**
* **Self-indulgence**
* **Gross consumerism**
* **Cult of the superwoman**

---

*Chart 42*

concluded by the Tennessee Valley Authority (TVA) which agreed to purchase from another power generator, Wisconsin Power & Light, the right to emit 10 000 tons of sulphur dioxide at $300 a ton. The cost to the TVA is obviously less than the installation of scrubbers to reduce sulphur dioxide emissions by 10 000 tons.

Reflecting the shifting priorities of contemporary times, there is a move in the world away from conspicuous consumption. This is epitomised in the US values which are on the upswing and downswing in the 1990s. The chrome bumpers of the 1950s, the psychedelic trips of the 1960s, the hard materialism of the 1970s and 1980s are being replaced by the understatement and puritanism of the 1990s. Inevitably the recession has bred more stoical attitudes in Western society. The yuppies are going to church for a change and have renamed themselves "guavas" – grown-up and vaguely ambitious. Across the ocean in England, the "hooray Henrys" are reverting to gardening: it's the fastest growth industry among the upper classes there. On both sides of the ocean aggressive feminism is making way for a feeling of confidence among women that the bars to their advancement are finally disappearing. As one female senator

---

**HEAVY TRENDS AND ATTITUDES**

**CONSUMPTION**
* Slowing desire to consume. Deconsumption
* Move away from ostentatious display
* Move away from hedonism/role models/life styles
* Move towards sharing/connections/emotions/ vitality
* Resistance to lack of creativity in product innovation
* More critical and selective attitude to advertising
* Japanese capacity of intraception. Deep reasons in their culture to look for and understand what people want

---

*Chart 43*

in the US said: "Any woman who wants to be equal to a man lacks ambition." Nevertheless, women's progress in business has not been nearly as spectacular as in, say, the legal profession. Only two per cent of boardroom positions in Britain and the US are occupied by women.

Arising out of the move away from ostentatious display, consumers are going to be a lot more discriminating in their choice of luxury goods in the 1990s. Sales of Rolls Royce cars in 1991 at 1723 were nearly half the previous year's number. Meanwhile the popularity of the Volkswagen Beetle, the "people's car", remains undiminished 21 million units later. To stay with the times the Japanese make a point of getting under the skin of their customers (intraception) to probe their deep-seated motives for purchasing their products. It pays off. Now that American cars are closing the gap with Japanese cars in terms of minimal reported defects, the Japanese are appealing to the senses of the American customer. The speed that a power window goes up and down, the "thunk" of a door as it closes, signal levers that cut like a knife, knobs that twist with no play – these are the features which the Japanese have discovered make all the difference in an American's purchasing decision. Interestingly, these qualities which appeal to the tactual and auditory senses are not obvious to the next-door neighbours, underlining the move away from explicit luxury.

Another trade-off which is hard to get right is the one involving economic development and quality of life. Many Americans today, with 37 per cent less leisure time than they had 20 years ago and a shrinking wilderness to relax in when they do have time off, feel their quality of life is declining. The Japanese prime minister, Kiichi Miyazawa, has set a new goal for Japan: a life-style superpower with particular emphasis on more living space and more leisure. Yet it's difficult to put the economic gears into reverse to try to reclaim an old way of living or create a revolutionary new one. An even more testing balance is the one between welfare and the incentive to work. It's perfectly reasonable to want to help people who are down on their luck and provide them with financial support to improve their quality of life. Hence the dole. But when the dole goes on for too long it corrodes the incentive to find a job and impairs economic performance. The hard liberal approach is an undying defence of individual liberty but an outright rejection of easy hand-outs of any kind – no protection for industry, no soft justice for criminals from disadvantaged backgrounds, no affirmative action and no way to obtain permanent welfare. The path of compensation (or reparation) to a hard liberal is the path to hell because it creates a dependency culture and thereby undermines economic development. The soft liberal would disagree, arguing that the weak and deprived are morally entitled to special treatment: it is not a matter where discretion can be exercised.

The balance of opinion in the Triad today is that special measures are required to assist those who are temporarily or permanently disadvantaged. These can include straight financial assistance where hardship can be proved, the onus of proof resting with the recipient. But the overwhelming type of assistance should be education and training leading to self-sufficiency as opposed to dependency. In this case, economic development and quality of life go hand in hand. The Swedes give generous unemployment pay for slightly over a year plus intensive training to anybody made redundant. Then the cash benefits are terminated, supplying the crucial incentive to go out and find a new job. Sweden's unemployment rate of 5,3 per cent is still well below the Triad average, although it is disappointingly double the rate of around 2 per cent which ruled until a year ago. It is a question of finding the right balance between the stick and the carrot.

A final story on values. I was a pupil at Winchester College in England, a high school renowned for its academic ethos. It therefore produced its fair share of youthful Effendis who wanted to change the world. A graffito scribbled on the wall of the college indicated our revolutionary tendencies by stating: "We are the children our parents warned us about." Anyway, my Latin master said to me when I was 16: "Clem, you may be a radical now but when you reach my age you'll end up in the soggy centre." I understand completely what he meant by that. As you get older you begin to capture the true richness of the world and you search for the golden mean in any situation. Tolerance and moderation become the two most important qualities of life.

## *"Winning Nation" and "Winning Company"*

The fourth "rule of the game" relates to "winning nations" and "winning companies". There are some who wish for the "international brotherhood of man", but the competitive nature of the world economy ensures that there will always be winners and losers. "Losing nations", however, used to be propped up by international aid and money lent by dewy-eyed bankers. The 1970s in particular were a time when the world's monetary system was awash with petro-dollars. Western banks fell over each other to on-lend the deposits of oil-producing nations to developing countries. Many Effendis became aid junkies, stringing out their careers on the donations received. The 1990s are different: a state of illiquidity exists in the world's capital markets. Countries seen as losers won't obtain a cent from any world institution or commercial bank. They will just drop off the radar screen. It is therefore even more imperative that people understand what it takes to be a "winning nation".

### *"Winning Nation"*

We have a portrait of a "winning nation" which, fortunately, is becoming familiar around the world. There are six conditions which have to be fulfilled.

### *Education*

The most important condition is education. Education more than any other factor determines the long-term fortunes of a nation. It is the source of progress, for the young man and woman who have an education can get a job. If they have a job, they can buy a house. And so it goes. The more knowledge intensive the world becomes, the more this principle will be reinforced.

As night follows day, the most educated countries are the most successful in the world. But it was always like this. When the Egyptians built the pyramids they were the most educated nation. When the Greeks invented democracy and those nasty geometrical theorems that you learn at school, they were the most educated. The Romans when they built the straight roads and the aqueducts had the best engineers. China's Sung dynasty with its emphasis on Confu-

**"WINNING NATION"**

* Education
* Work ethic
* High savings rate
* "Dual-logic" economy
* Social harmony
* Global player

*Chart 44*

cian-style education produced great cities, successful traders, cannons and gunpowder. The Spanish, the Dutch and the Portuguese when they discovered the world had the best navigators. The British at the time of the Industrial Revolution had the best scientists. Many people believe that Britain owes its greatness to its aristocracy and military leaders. Not a bit of it. Britain's golden era in the 19th Century is rooted in the "dissenting academies" of the preceding century; these were church schools in England and Wales with a broader curriculum than the grammar schools at the time. In particular they encouraged the study of experimental science. In so doing they influenced the teaching methods of the great grammar schools of the 19th Century. Sad to say, the majority of the latter were abolished some 30 years ago on the ground that they were too elite to be state schools. The British educational system produced geniuses such as James Hargreaves (spinning-jenny), James Watt (steam engine) and George Stephenson (steam locomotive). These inventions paved the way for Britain's manufacturing prowess in the reign of Queen Victoria. Meanwhile Britain's public schools such as Eton and Harrow were responsible for the mandarins who ran the British Empire. But that empire would never have existed without the simple, practical men who built and operated the cotton and steel mills.

Germany and America followed Britain in the 19th and 20th Centuries, but now the most educated nation on earth is the Japanese. Very few nations come close to the Japanese. Any science or mathematics olympiad their schoolchildren participate in they win:

91

only the Taiwanese and South Koreans (and the Chinese in maths) come close. It is said that the average Japanese schoolchild is some one to two years ahead of his American counterpart. But it's not just any old education system in Japan; it's one that is designed for the social and economic needs of Japan. The average entrance grades to Japanese technical schools are similar to those in their grammar schools. One of the best statistics for judging whether a nation is going up or down is the number of engineers per lawyer. In Japan they produce engineers, in America they produce lawyers. Japan's slogan these days is: "Knowledge is power." Ideas conquer the world now, not armies. To adapt an old expression, power flows through the barrel of a pen, not through the barrel of a gun. Japan regards its education system as its invisible asset.

Germany, like Japan, focuses on vocational education. Two-thirds of German schoolchildren go into some form of practical skills training at the age of 16. This overlaps seamlessly with the apprenticeship system and other industrial training later on. German engineering skills are considered among the finest in the world. What Japan and Germany have both avoided is the pitfall of having a good education system which churns out unemployable intellectuals who have no choice but to become Effendis of the negative kind. Canada has introduced "co-op" education, where classroom instruction is alternated with on-the-job training. Obviously one is not arguing for education that produces youthful industrial robots. The humanities are vital for a child's rounded development. Yet again, it is a question of balance. On the one hand an appreciation of the arts is vital to quality of life, but on the other hand life has no quality without some level of material prosperity produced by technological advancement.

In contrast to Japan and Germany, the American story is a sad one of declining standards at schools even though they still have the best universities in the world. SAT verbal scores have consistently declined over the last 20 years. Mathematics results have held up principally because of an influx of high-scoring Asian American students from the mid-1980s onwards. Among children beginning high school the United States is well behind South Korea and Taiwan in proficiency in both mathematics and science. As the first annual

# EDUCATION IN THE UNITED STATES

SAT scores for college-bound students

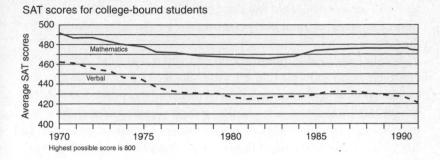

Highest possible score is 800

Mathematics proficiency among 13-year-olds, 1990-91

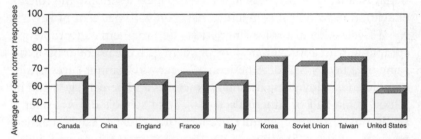

Science proficiency among 13-year-olds, 1990-91

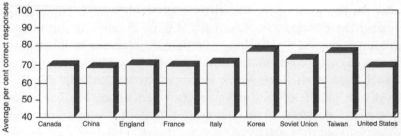

SOURCE: First Annual Report of US Competitiveness Policy Council, March 1992

*Chart 45*

report of the Competitiveness Policy Council to the President and Congress said in March 1992: "US education performance is inadequate by any conceivable standard . . . The goal must be a restoration of globally competitive performance by American students by 2000."

Another noticeable point about educational comparisons is the relatively good showing of the former Soviet Union. Given the dismal economic performance of the republics when they formed the Soviet Union, this fact signifies that a high educational standard is a necessary but not a sufficient condition for economic progress. It has to be combined with all the other features that make up a "winning nation".

Three shocking points were made by the President of the US National Academy of Sciences in a recent paper describing the role of education in technical competitiveness: only 40 per cent of American 13-year-olds can solve simple two-step mathematics problems, compared with approximately 78 per cent of Korean children of the same age; nearly half of American 17-year-olds cannot successfully complete tasks involving decimals, fractions and percentages; and in 1986 almost half of America's 16 000 high schools did not offer a single physics course, mainly because they did not have qualified teachers, while 4 200 schools had no chemistry course and 1 900 schools no biology course. The American educational Effendis must take partial responsibility for the deterioration in educational standards. In the spirit of the Woodstock 1960s they have campaigned against the classic ways of formally drilling children in arithmetic, grammar, vocabulary, spelling and diction in favour of inculcating habits of social co-operation and equality. Discipline was replaced by self-expression. Tests which separated the academically excellent from the middle-of-the-road were frowned upon. No marks, no streaming, no stress. Teaching course content was less important than instilling the capacity to "conceptualise" and "problem solve". Social studies outrated science, commerce and the acquisition of job-related skills. The result is a mush of semiremembered facts and semiunderstood concepts in the minds of too many children. No wonder US companies complain bitterly about the quality not of their managerial intake from universities and business schools but much of their run-of-the-mill intake from high schools. Often they provide bridging courses themselves to these recruits to overcome the deficiencies of the general education system. Britain has followed the same sad route.

One senses now a determination in both countries to reverse the experiments of the last 20 years and to get back to basics in the classroom. The uptick in US productivity in the 1980s confirms America's change of heart. But the pendulum will never swing fully back on teaching methods, nor indeed should it. A golden mean applies in the classroom as it does elsewhere. Teach children the benefits of both competition and co-operation. Be strict, but give sufficient space for the nurturing of independent initiative. The Japanese are moving to the centre from the other pole of too much conformity and too little recreation in their schools.

No education system will work properly unless you pay the teachers well. Highly educated graduates queue up in Japan for teaching posts because teachers are in the top quartile of income earners. Alas, in the United States and Britain the quality of the teaching profession is declining because the good people vote with their feet out of the profession and into industry for better salaries, particularly those qualified in mathematics and science. Yet in Japan they spend 3,5 per cent of Gross National Product on education compared with Britain's 5 per cent and America's 12 per cent. How can the Japanese get away with it, and pay their teachers well? The answer is they have the smallest civil service in the world. They have the smallest number of Effendis per teacher in the classroom. There isn't that huge amorphous mass of school inspectors, educational liaison officers and other administrators who have to be paid before you pay the frontline troops who actually do the teaching. Thus it's important for the US and Britain to streamline their education systems so as to release money from overheads and top up the salaries of the teachers themselves. As Japan has shown, just throwing money at education (or health for that matter) does not necessarily improve your position relative to other countries. It's better management that counts.

At the same time, granting more autonomy to schools (and to hospitals) seems to work, as does giving more choice to parents as to which school they send their children. The Catholic schools and the "magnet" schools in the US and the schools that have opted out of local authority control in England are the ones showing superior performance. In 1974 East Harlem in New York was 32nd out of 32 school districts in terms of its results. By 1988 it had climbed to eighth position largely because of the introduction of "magnet" schools. They allow the people who know the local conditions – the principal, teachers and parents – to have more control over the school's affairs. They recruit the teachers, decide the salaries and choose the most appropriate teaching methods within the boundaries of a national or state curriculum. They even have special levies on the parents to finance capital developments such as a new hall or sports field or to provide a subvention to teachers they really want to keep. Furthermore, with decentralisation the local community can hold the teaching staff accountable for the results of the school. No principal can shrug his shoulders at poor results and blame it on "the system".

An even more radical approach would be to abandon zoning of any kind. Instead the state would issue vouchers to all parents which they could cash on behalf of their children at the school of their choice. Additional money would flow to those schools with the best performances in examinations, putting pressure on inefficient schools to change their teaching methods or face closure. As in business, the spur of competition and the fear of bankruptcy might well result in the customer getting what he or she wants: a decent education for the children which, among other things, increases their chances of finding a job afterwards. As one proponent of the voucher system argued: "If nationalised industry doesn't work, why should nationalised education?"

The thinking behind the voucher system is not new. In the 12th and 13th Centuries the University of Bologna did not pay its professors a salary. Instead, the professors each had a collection box at their lectures into which students were invited to make a donation after the lecture was over.

The second condition for a "winning nation" is a work ethic. Surprise, surprise – you have to work hard to win. And we found four prerequisites for a work ethic. The most important is "small government". Experience everywhere since the Second World War conclusively proves that undergoverned people generate wealth and income more quickly than overgoverned people.

Look at the Taiwanese versus the mainland Chinese; South Koreans versus North Koreans; West Germans versus East Germans: same people, different systems of government. The undergoverned win every time because bureaucracy sucks the creative lifeblood out of people. For this reason the divine authority chose not to be a central planner – by giving us all "free will". But let's go to the horse's mouth of a Russian Effendi of the positive kind. Here is an excerpt from an article written by Nikolai Shmelyov in the Soviet magazine *Novy Mir* or *New World* at the beginning of 1988. "Persistent long-term efforts to overturn the objective laws of economic life and crush the age-old incentives to work have brought results directly opposite to those we had anticipated . . . Massive apathy, indifference, disrespect for honest labour, together with aggressive envy towards those who earn more, have led to signs of degradation of a significant part of the people . . . Salaries and bonuses don't work because there is nothing for the people to buy with their money . . . We need to permit companies and organisations to sell freely, to buy and borrow, in place of fruitless efforts at central planning. We need to realise that there is such a thing as natural unemployment. The real possibility of losing one's job, of being forced to move to a new place of employment, is not at all bad medicine . . . The economic situation will have to depend directly on profit, and profit cannot fulfil its function until prices are liberated from subsidies. Over the centuries, humankind has found no more effective measure of work than profit. Our suspicious attitude towards profit is a misunderstanding, the cost of the economic illiteracy of people who thought that socialism would eliminate profit and loss . . . Consumers need to have both rights and opportunities to take what is offered or turn it down. That means they have to have a real choice . . . Bottom-line market stimuli must extend to all states of the research, development, investment, production, marketing and service process."

Nobody can be so eloquent about the shortcomings of "big government" as someone who's lived under it. The less a government interferes in the lives of ordinary, law-abiding citizens, the better it is. That doesn't mean the government doesn't have a role to play. Of course it does – in education, health, defence, law and order, infrastructure, fiscal policy and the maintenance of a competitive business environment (Europe's long-distance telephone calls are four times as expensive as America's, due to lack of competition). So we don't mean weak government by "small government". Government must perform a limited role competently. Paradoxically, benevolent forms of government intervention actually increase individual liberty. Educated healthy people have more freedom of choice than ignorant sick people – hence the provision by the state of money to underwrite free education and health care is a positive action. The best analogy I can submit of the role government ought to play is that of game rangers who behind the scenes ensure that the game park is kept in optimum condition for its inhabitants to lead their natural lives. Visitors go to the game park to see the game, not the rangers: likewise, governments are the servants of the people – not the other way round. The media have a lot to answer for with their obsession with politics – it gives politicians far too grand an idea of their station in life. After all, a politician is defined as a person who watches which way the crowd is moving and then jumps out in front and says "follow me"!

One last aspect of "small government" which has caught the headlines since the initial sale of British Telecom shares in 1984 has been privatisation. Apart from raising $250 billion for the governments concerned, has it worked? A recent World Bank study looked at three cases in each of four countries – Britain, Mexico, Malaysia and Chile – and concluded that in 11 of the 12 examples there had been an overall gain. Improved efficiencies and the freedom to make commercial investment decisions were cited as two of the key reasons for the success of privatisation. The industries covered by the study comprised three telecommunication firms, four airlines, two electricity utilities, a road haulier, a container port and a lottery business.

The second prerequisite for a work ethic is a low tax regime. Since tax is raised to pay for government expenditure, this entails low government expenditure. For a developing country, government expenditure should not be much more than 20 per cent of Gross National Product and should never exceed 30 per cent. This is an exceedingly tough target given the priorities of education, health, etc. But a small business cannot afford a large head office. Thailand is running at around 17 per cent and Singapore close to 20 per cent. For developed countries, which have gone through the "fast growth" phase and are rich enough to afford it, government expenditure ranges from 30 per cent of the Gross National Product for Japan and Switzerland to 40 per cent for Britain to the upper 50s for Sweden and Denmark (the last two having every intention of reducing their ratios).

Governments everywhere have been lowering rates of income tax, because people work harder if they keep the money they earn in their back pockets. In addition, the lesson has been learnt that if you tax the successful too much they emigrate. The top rate of income tax in the US has come down from 70 per cent to 31 per cent and in Britain from 83 per cent to 40 per cent. But one mustn't just look at the maximum rate: the level at which it is applied is also of relevance. A married person hits the top rate at $1^{1}/_{2}$ times average earnings in Britain; in the US it's four times average earnings. In France and Germany (which have higher maximum rates of 57 per cent and 53 per cent respectively) it's six times average earnings. It is important that the top rate does not apply too soon.

To compensate for the loss of income from the lowering of income tax rates, but mindful of the fact that high corporate taxes discourage new business investment by local and foreign firms, governments are resorting to a value added tax (VAT). Britain's VAT is currently 17,5 per cent on the majority of goods and services produced. While gathering revenue in this fashion is less harmful than steepening the income tax gradient, such taxes can add to inflation. Moreover, along with state and municipal taxes VAT will obviously be figured into any calculation of final take-home pay by people whose professional qualifications give them the flexibility of deciding which country they should live in. Another drawback of VAT is that it can impact heavily on the poor if exemptions aren't given on basic foods and medicines.

Even the application of VAT may not provide sufficient additional income for some governments to continue in their profligate ways. In the old days they printed money to make up the difference, which was highly inflationary. To foreclose that option many central banks have become more independent of governmental authority. So governments now borrow money to pay for the deficit between their ingoings and outgoings. While in the short term the result may not be misery (to use Mr Micawber's expression) in the longer run it certainly is, particularly when the money is being borrowed to finance current administration expenditure as opposed to capital investment. The Italian government's debt is now more than 100 per cent of Gross National Product and its annual borrowing requirement 11 per cent. Much of the money raised merely repays the interest on the total outstanding debt. The parlous financial state that the Italian government has got itself into is the principal reason for the phenomenal rise in the popularity of the Northern League, a party based in Milan and led by Umberto Bossi. They secured 20 per cent of the vote in Lombardy and nearly 9 per cent of the vote nationwide in the general election in April 1992. Their platform is that Rome is not only financially incompetent, but milking the richer north to win popularity in the poorer south. They want Italy to become three self-governing macroregions. To them, Italy as a whole is a club that has lost its value. Moreover, with Italy in mind, the European Community's leaders at their Maastricht summit in December 1991 made it a condition of progress towards union that the budget deficits of member governments should be less than 3 per cent of Gross Domestic Product.

The American Congress has the same problem with deficits. US Government debt is about 60 per cent of Gross National Product, while the deficit to be financed by borrowings has inexorably risen to around 7 per cent. This squeezes the savings market domestically and overseas, because an annual borrowing requirement of $400 billion is large by even the standards of the international capital market. The Congressional Effendis won't cut their own expenditure, but neither do they possess the courage to raise taxes to balance the books. Either way costs votes. It shows the utter mess which arises from promoting the philosophy of entitlements from

# UNITED STATES BUDGET DEFICIT

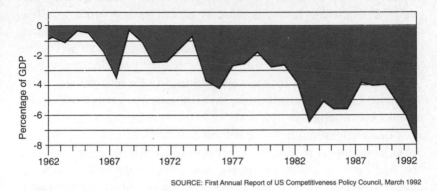

SOURCE: First Annual Report of US Competitiveness Policy Council, March 1992

*Chart 46*

the centre in order to curry short-term popularity with the electorate.

Sweden offers the most dramatic example of a country that has woken up to the fact that high taxes kill the work ethic. Once touted as the "third way" between capitalism and socialism, Sweden is opting for a much reduced welfare system and more moderate taxes to reinvigorate its economy.

The message is simple and clear: "small government" with lean administration costs will effectively answer the question of how much you should tax the rich and the poor.

The third prerequisite for a work ethic is a sound family system. In the Far East it's considered honourable to be a housewife and raise children, so the family is held together. In the West the status of the family has declined with appalling consequences. There are now one million people in US jails out of a population of 240 million. One in every 240 Americans is in jail. It's the highest incarceration rate in the world, and – some may say – a tribute to the powers of detection of their police force. But it's not just about increasing the number of "cops" on the beat and building more jails. In Britain, expenditure on law and order went up by 40 per cent in real terms during the 1980s but recorded crime rose by 50 per cent. No, it goes deeper than that. You have latch-key children who let themselves into empty homes, you have children who don't even know who

101

their parents are. They seek elsewhere the identity they should have been given in their family. They join gangs. They peddle drugs. The vacuum of the lost family is filled by crime. As one young gunman said when explaining his motives for random shooting of pedestrians: "I kill, therefore I am." The fundamental unit of society is the family, and if a country wants to be a "winning nation" it must respect that statement. It you want children to be responsible, hardworking and really contribute to the common weal, they must have a sound upbringing.

The fourth prerequisite for a work ethic is clean government. The best prescription to combat corruption is a multiparty democracy backed up by a totally free press: not a "reasonably" free press as some would have it. As soon as the word "reasonably" is interposed, a subjective form of censorship is immediately being applied. After all, "reasonable" in media terms normally means flattering to me but critical of my opponents. If someone feels he has been hard done by in the media, recourse to the courts is always there. The combination of democracy plus a free press is the only way to expose a political party when it is corrupt, and to limit its days in office by voting it out at the next election.

Having said all that, a third and somewhat surprising condition also pertains for clean government. The public must actively wish to use the prerogative it has in removing dishonest politicians. Otherwise democracy doesn't work that well. In the US, the recent exposé of Congressmen writing out cheques for more than their balances permitted at the House bank ("Rubbergate") and the regular tales of crookery by state and municipal officials show that the media are doing their job. But somehow the corruption never seems to diminish. It is almost as if the American public expect political Effendis to feather their own nests. Yet they have only themselves to blame for this sleaze, because they have the capacity – through their vote – to enforce a much higher level of morality on the world of politics. A sardonic observation by one city dweller probably says it all: "Corruption is better than incompetence. Bribery at least gets things done."

If the US is bad Japan is worse, given the recent spate of property and share scandals involving politicians. This may be a reflection of the entrenched position of the ruling party. Although Japanese society has been shaken to the core by the extent of corruption in its midst, this distress is unlikely to lead to a change of party at the helm. There is the matter of saving face, which means that any government or corporate official dismissed for serious misdemeanours commonly reappears somewhere else after an appropriate period of penitence.

Notwithstanding the unsatisfactory state of affairs in the US and Japan, and in some European countries as well, the Triad is well down the corruption league compared to developing countries. In many of the latter a corruption syndrome reigns which is almost impossible to root out. One cannot even say that the economic stars have been less corrupt than some of the laggards. Thailand has been the fastest growing economy in the world, but public disgust over graft in high places has recently propelled Chamlong Srimuang, a devout Buddhist who was Governor of Bangkok for six years, into being Thailand's most popular politician. He has vowed to sweep out rotten administration and substitute honest, efficient government.

So why add "clean government" as a condition for a "winning nation" when so many winners patently aren't clean? The reason, apart from the strong ethical argument against corruption, is that a bribe is no more and no less than an invisible tax on honestly earned income and, as we know, high taxes neutralise the work ethic. A sick society will eventually collapse under its own venality. Moreover, to turn the situation around requires more than vigilant auditors and draconian laws. It goes back to the basic values passed on by parents to their children.

The current weakening of the work ethic in Germany shows how hard it is to maintain employee motivation at a high level when you have years of success behind you. Germans now work 1 647 hours on average per year compared to 1 904 in the US and 2 175 for Japanese. Germans are entitled to six weeks' leave plus 11 public holidays a year. On top of that the average German employee is on sick leave for 145 hours a year, compared to 57 hours for Americans and 36 hours for Japanese. It works out at $2^{1}/_{2}$ months' paid absence per year for the German worker. Chancellor Kohl sums it up by saying that Germany has become a vacationer's republic. But that is not all. In 1991 West Germany's hourly wage in manufacturing was $22,32 against $15,38 in the United States and $14,22 in Japan.

Like any modern society, Germany is a combination of world-class companies seeking to retain their competitive edge in world markets, and powerful trade unions wanting the best for their members. If the latter push their demands too far, real wages will eventually fall as firms go out of business and unemployment rises. The line between the affordable and the not affordable is often very fine but the Germans seem clearly to have crossed it, going in the wrong direction.

### High Savings Rate

The third condition for a "winning nation" is a high savings rate. There is an old macroeconomic equation you cannot get around: "Savings equal investment." If people don't save, you can't invest in the future of your country. In the Far East they save 15 to 20 per cent of personal income, in Italy they save 26 per cent, in the US only 5 per cent. It means the Americans are going to have to be weaned away from the spend-now-save-later outlook on life.

Japanese and German households have consistently saved more than American households in the 15 years from 1975 to 1990. So net private investment of the two countries has consistently outstripped America's as a percentage of Gross Domestic Product. The flip side of a spendthrift society is that total US business, household and government debt has soared to 200 per cent of Gross National Product. I may sound like an old-fashioned Calvinist, but sensible people put money aside for a rainy day: they don't hock themselves up to the eyeballs. These statistics also debunk the conspiracy theory, namely that a handful of ultra-rich Americans meet in New York once a month to decide on the future direction of the world. If there was to be a meeting, it would be in Tokyo or Taipei, where the real money resides.

High inflation, the scourge of many developing countries, destroys a savings habit. People question the wisdom of putting money on deposit at the bank only to see it fall in value in real terms, so they spend their salaries and wages as soon as they receive them. Ideally the interest rate on deposits (after tax) should consistently exceed

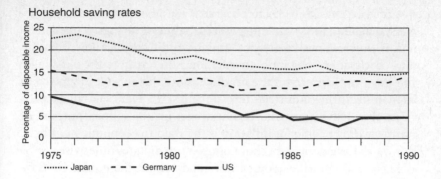

Household saving rates

........ Japan    - - - Germany    ▬▬ US

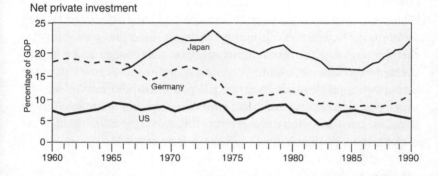

Net private investment

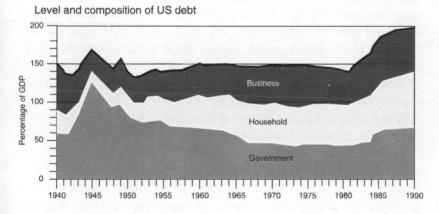

Level and composition of US debt

SOURCE: First Annual Report of US Competitiveness Policy Council, March 1992

*Chart 47*

the inflation rate, in order to provide a genuine incentive for the average person to forgo consumption in favour of savings. That condition is much easier to achieve under conditions of a low inflation rate. The sole remedy for high inflation is to return to the old adage: you pay people more if they produce more. Japan's wage growth in its manufacturing industries has in the last 25 years seldom exceeded its productivity growth. Raising wages for the solitary purpose of compensating people for inflation is the road to economic perdition. But we all have done it, because conscience dictates otherwise.

There is one further point to be made about the equation "Savings equal investment". It is not just the amount of investment that counts, it is also the quality. As any businessman knows, you can invest wisely and multiply your fortune or you can fritter your money away on lousy decisions. It is not predetermined that a new investment creates wealth. Investments must be well chosen and well implemented. Hence a country's having a high ratio of investment to Gross National Product does not tell you the whole story. The former Soviet Union invested huge sums on industrial plant over many decades, but the nation grew poorer. Private sector investment is invariably more profitable than public sector investment.

### "Dual-logic" Economy

The fourth condition for a "winning nation" is a "dual-logic" economy. You need big business with high technology and financial resources to undertake the big projects in a country and compete with the other giants in the world. But underpinning big business you need a thriving small business and informal sector, because that's where most of the jobs are going to be created and that is the birthplace of the future stars of big business.

Both sides march to a different drum, hence the expression "dual-logic". Big business inevitably needs greater co-ordination and more sophisticated internal control mechanisms to keep the show on the road. The more complex an organisation becomes, the more it has to be managed with certain set standards and procedures. To entrepreneurs setting up their own businesses, such talk sounds positively Effendi-ish. They need minimum controls, maximum flexibility and dead-simple operating and reporting systems.

106

Where a profitable relationship between big business and small business develops, an economic miracle can happen. In Japan it was the video cassette recorder that Sony and small business designed jointly. In the United States it's the retail franchise industry, the fastest-growing part of the retail sector. Combining the brand name and marketing, accounting and inventory skills of big business with the raw entrepreneurialism of the individual shop-owner yields a very potent package. It also provides a greater chance of success in that 90 US franchises out of 100 are still going strong after 10 years compared to 16 out of 100 small businesses generally.

In the Far East they've developed a concept called the centre-satellite system. The company at the centre is usually larger and more established than the rest: it co-ordinates the manufacturing process and does the final assembly work of the consumer product. In turn that company sub-contracts the manufacture of specific components to microbusinesses (often one-man bands) with highly focused skills. Take a simple product like cutlery. The handle of a knife will be shaped by one firm, the blade by another, the two being put together by a bigger brother who markets the object. Overheads are kept to a minimum.

In the West, following the lead given in the public relations field, a growth industry has been companies contracting themselves as human resources departments to businesses that want to shed that function. The outside specialist leases the staff to the business, thereby becoming the employer of record for tax and insurance purposes. The responsibility for administering the payroll, medical benefits, unemployment insurance, etc, is hived off to an expert. This is a special example of a more general trend where big businesses are shrinking their organisations to a central core of highly productive primary employees and contracting all other tasks out. Not only does this allow them to concentrate entirely on the product or service they have to offer, it also provides them with greater flexibility in coping with the peaks and troughs of the business cycle. Temporary staff are contracted in and shed, as and when the level of activity demands it.

In essence, large organisations are privatising their non-essential functions, passing them on to smaller firms. They have woken up to the fact that largeness can bring diseconomies of scale through superfluous overheads which small firms don't carry. At IBM a third of the price of a computer is absorbed in marketing, administration and service overheads. Hence the shake-up. In the British civil service the intention of the mandarins is to sub-contract nearly a third of the routine work to outsiders. One day you may have hospitals that only diagnose and cure, universities that only teach – all the paraphernalia of administration which doctors and professors hate anyway being tendered for in the market. That's "dual-logic".

### Social Harmony

The fifth condition for a "winning nation" is social harmony. After all, if you have one half of a nation trying to kill the other half of a nation you can't possibly be a "winning nation". Prime examples are the wars between rival clans in Mogadishu and between the Mujahedin in "liberated" Kabul. It is unlikely that either Somalia or Afghanistan will become a "winning nation" in the near future. Lebanon was the centre of commerce in the Middle East until Beirut was destroyed. People have to get along with one another, but that doesn't mean making daily declarations of love to one another in a sickly-sweet manner. It means having a strong sense of social justice running through society – a feeling that the system is fair. A clear and respected legal code, good company law, a stable tax and investment regime: these are the backbone of a prosperous business community. Theodore Roosevelt said in 1904: "If America is to be a permanently good place for each of us to live in, it must be a reasonably good place for all of us to live in." That statement is as relevant today as it was in 1904. Alas, America failed to abide by the principle. It now has a 20 per cent underclass who live outside the mainstream of society and are a great source of instability. One hundred years ago, America *was* middle class. Now it *has* a middle class, as well as an upper and lower class.

The incredible performance by the four Asian dragons has raised an interesting debate. None of them was a democracy during their economic lift-off. China itself, which has been no slouch recently in terms of economic growth (8 to 10 per cent per annum), is still a totalitarian state. Chile in South America reverted from a democratically elected head of state to a general before its era of economic prosperity started. On the other side of the fence, India is a prime example of a democratic country which has under-performed, although there are promising signs of change. The argument goes that to climb the initial rungs of the economic ladder requires a degree of self-sacrifice and hardship that a democracy won't tolerate. Furthermore, it is only when prosperity is fairly well distributed that a democratic culture sets in. Hence the only way to maintain social harmony in the early years of transition is by authoritarian government. The final conclusion is that a "winning nation" should initially be led by a benevolent dictator.

Powerful stuff, but it ignores probably the most important aspect of social harmony: human dignity. The recent riots in Bangkok show how brittle society in an Asian dragon really is. People have to possess self-esteem if they are to give of their best. But then they must feel part and parcel of the community in which they live. This in turn means having not only a sense of freedom about one's own affairs but a sense of sharing in the direction of the community's affairs as well. That leads to only one conclusion: a universal franchise. As history has shown, the extension of the franchise, wherever it has occurred, has pre-empted Karl Marx's revolutionary scenario because there are no alienated masses to inflame.

However, there is one crucial qualification, which is why the Russian transition to free enterprise and democracy is so dangerous. While economic growth does not have to precede political liberation, it has to accompany it. Democracy can very quickly turn to anarchy – which gives an excuse for a new dictator to fill the vacuum – if widespread social unrest prevails because of poor living conditions and unemployment. Robespierre, when facing the guillotine in 1794, lamented thus to the French peasants: "I gave you freedom: now you want bread as well." The modern equivalent is jobs. Spain and Portugal made a successful transition to open societies because their economic fortunes improved at the same time. Income per head in Spain has risen from 60 per cent of the European Community's average in 1960 to 75 per cent in 1980 to 80 per cent in 1991. The gap is closing, the Spanish are happy (King Juan Carlos has also been a brilliant facilitator).

Karl Marx said: "It is not the consciousness of men which determines their existence; it is on the contrary their social existence which determines their consciousness." His proposition has been fulfilled in a way that he would never have imagined. The governments of Western countries took a leaf out of his book. They enfranchised the working classes; they provided them with free education and free hospitals. More recently they have encouraged widespread home- and share-ownership. They generally improved the quality of life of the common man and woman by facilitating their entry into the mainstream of society. Result: members of the working class, when given the opportunity, dropped all ideas of a revolution in favour of pursuing their individual occupations and becoming members of the middle class themselves. Democracy Western-style has proved to be an unbeatable moderating force. It is the most powerful paradigm in the world today. No country is ever criticised for having too much democracy. It is part of the Second Reformation. Rulers ignore this fact at their peril but there are many who still do.

Case closed: the optimum state is political and economic liberation – hand in hand. And "winning nations" only aim for the best, and help others to do that too.

### Global Player

The last condition for a "winning nation" is that you have to be a global player. You have to look outwards. You must regard the world economy as your oyster. There are no borders to your ambition. You should have the *chutzpah* to say: "I am going to produce certain products in my country which are going to take the world by storm." Outward-looking economies grow three times faster than inward-looking economies, according to a recent World Bank survey: 7,5 per cent versus 2,5 per cent per annum. It stands to reason why. When you're outward-looking you're taking advantage of your unique strengths to export to the rest of the world; when you're inward-looking you're producing some products you should never be producing in the first place because somebody else can do it better. Even a giant like the US has become increasingly dependent on the world economy: international trade has increased from 11 per cent of Gross National Product in 1960 to 25 per cent in 1990. However,

110

the success of countries like Taiwan shows that you don't have to be a giant to establish a profitable niche in world markets. Taiwan is really a thriving network of medium-sized and small businesses with highly ambitious, outward-looking entrepreneurs in the driving seats. Germany has been like this for a long time with its "hidden champions", small companies which have dominant world market shares in niche products such as bottling machines and food for tropical fish, but which are relatively unknown even in Germany itself.

It is almost impossible to have an outward-looking economy if it is protected at the same time. Protection raises the input costs of your exporters, making them less competitive in world markets. Exporters must be free to import from the lowest cost sources in the world without having to pay duties or tariffs. Freedom of movement of foreign exchange is equally important. Flows either way provide an excellent yardstick of whether the government is doing a good job in turning the country into a global player.

### The Current Scorecard

Let's repeat the six conditions for a "winning nation": education, work ethic, high savings rate, a "dual-logic" economy, social harmony and being a global player. How do the three core members of the Triad and the Asian dragons shape up to this definition? I've constructed a table where points on a scale of 0 to 1 are awarded for

### SCORECARD FOR "WINNING NATIONS"

|  | US | Japan | Western Europe | Asian Dragons |
|---|---|---|---|---|
| Education | 1/2 | 7/8 | 3/4 | 3/4 |
| Work ethic | 3/4 | 7/8 | 1/2 | 1 |
| High savings rate | 1/4 | 1 | 1/2 | 1 |
| "Dual-logic" economy | 1/2 | 3/4 | 1/2 | 3/4 |
| Social harmony | 1/2 | 3/4 | 1/2 | 1/4 |
| Global player | 1 | 3/4 | 1/2 | 1/2 |

*Chart 48*

each characteristic of a "winning nation" – 0 is dreadful and 1 is excellent. Although such ratings are highly subjective, and in this case reflect my opinion, it is an illuminating exercise in comparing the strengths and weaknesses of the main players in the Triad game (the figures are certainly too subjective to add up to a total).

To start with I've awarded America's educational system $\frac{1}{2}$ because it represents a mixed bag. On the one hand it has schools that need improving, but on the other it has universities which in many cases are world-class centres of excellence and attract the best research skills from all other countries. From the point of view of the mass of the population, though, it is the quality of schooling that is important. Education in the Asian dragons is at least abreast of Europe, particularly in science and mathematics, but neither has the generally high standard of Japan's schools. European and American universities are on a par with and in some cases outrank Japanese universities. For this reason Japan didn't receive an outright 1. In regard to work ethic, the US outranks Europe but Japan is ahead of them both with a question mark over the attitude of the next generation. The Asian dragons are still at the "lean and hungry" stage of achieving economic success.

The US savings rate is poor, Europe's is good to fair depending on which country you choose, while the Far East on the whole enjoys an excellent savings ethic. Neither the US nor Europe has explored fully the concept of a "dual-logic" economy, as can be seen by the way the industrial giants in the two regions have only recently tumbled to the idea of a high degree of decentralisation whereby non-essential activities will be contracted out. Japan and the Asian dragons are far more advanced in their development of links between big and small business. As for social harmony, neither America nor Europe can be given a higher rating than $\frac{1}{2}$ for different reasons: America because of a significant underclass and Europe because of national rivalries (individual European countries would deserve more than $\frac{1}{2}$). The Asian dragons are very brittle and in many instances still have a long way to go to be classified as open democracies. Japan, one senses, is growing tired of "one-party rule". The bubble of a soaring market in shares and property – "Tokyo-mania" – has burst and the repercussions will be felt in Japanese society for a long time.

Nevertheless, Japan has been given a higher rating than America and Europe on the grounds of being an homogenous society and pervasively middle class. It is also the least litigious!

In respect of the final characteristic of being a global player, the United States, despite surrendering its massive lead over the rest of the world, remains the leader of the pack. Unlike others before it, it is a nation examining its flaws while it is still strong. It retains an indomitable spirit and prodigious energy: when needs must, it can renew itself. America's absolute productivity level is 10 to 15 per cent higher than Japan's and is now growing as fast (after an indifferent period from 1960 to the mid-1980s). Its volume of merchandise exports doubled between 1983 and 1991, nearly half of the new jobs created in export industries during those years being in manufacturing. In terms of competitiveness the US can still produce the best in the world whether it's Boeing with aircraft, Microsoft with software or Hollywood with movies. Whatever faults there are with America – and the education system has to be the chief area of concern – the last thing one wants to happen is for its citizens to lose their confidence and turn inwards.

Japan is the economic crown prince, although by its high standards of economic performance the last few years have been disastrous. The Japanese flagship companies in cameras, computers, computer chips and consumer electronics are experiencing a torrid time because of the world recession, some reporting profit drops of over 50 per cent. However, their superior manufacturing practices and systems of innovation are still very much in place. It is more in the non-economic sphere that Japan has plenty to learn before receiving the accolade of superpower status. The difference between a truly great nation and a "winning nation" is that the former has the additional trait of helping other countries to become winners in their own right. America at times has gone out of its way to do that: Japan hasn't. Europe and the Asian dragons have been accorded a lower rating than the United States and Japan, the former because one must have doubts about Europe's ability to stay at the cutting edge of high technology and the latter because the Asian dragons are still in a catch-up phase with Japan. It still has to be seen whether they can develop into original sources of technological innovation.

So pervasive are the new information and communication technologies (ICT) that older management structures geared to the previous waves of technology are gradually adapting themselves to take full advantage of ICT. Moreover, the days of the "electronic heroin trail" when pushy computer salesmen hooked companies on far more sophisticated programmes and hardware than they actually required are over.

The development of ICT and microelectronics has gone hand in hand. As mainframe computers are overshadowed by ever more versatile personal computers, so centralised information systems are making way for local area networks offering distributed intelligence. This in turn leads to a change in a company's paradigm to make it compatible with ICT. "Winning companies" will be those that ride the ICT wave for all it is worth. For several centuries, fortunes have been made by people who profited from having systems which obtained important news first. The only difference now is that ICT is the modern equivalent of the carrier pigeon, the mounted courier and the telegraph.

What other features does a "winning company" have? First and foremost, as a "winning nation" has a high standard of education so the company that spends time and money on training and develop-

---

**A "WINNING COMPANY"**

* Adapts to the ICT wave
* Considers training central to the business
* Has a lean head office
* Sees technological innovation as a random process
* Starts with what the customer can afford in feasibility studies
* Stresses ethics as well as profits
* Pioneers new markets in developing countries

---

*Chart 49*

## CHANGE OF TECHNO-PARADIGM

| "FORDIST" OLD | ICT NEW |
|---|---|
| Energy-intensive | Information-intensive |
| Standardised | Customised |
| Rather stable product mix | Rapid changes in product mix |
| Dedicated plant and equipment | Flexible production systems |
| Acceptance of rejects as normal | High quality and zero defects as goals |
| Automation | Systemation |
| Product with service | Service with products |
| Single firm | Networks |
| Hierarchical structures | Flat horizontal structures |
| Departmental | Integrated |
| Centralisation | Distributed intelligence |
| Specialised skills | Multi-skilling |
| Minimise training requirements | Continuous training and retraining |
| Adversarial industrial relations. Collective agreements codify provisional armistices | Moves towards long-term consultative and participative industrial relations |
| "Full employment" (emphasis on full-time employment for adult (16-55) male workers) | "Active society" (more flexible hours and involvement of part-time workers and post-retirement people) |

*Chart 50*

ing its workforce is the one that will succeed. Plant and technology are easily transferable – people are not. It is from people, more than any other resource, that a company derives its unique strength. Besides, a mind is a "terrible thing to waste".

Many Western organisations pay lip service to training, sending their workers away on courses and never following up afterwards. The job and the course are separate entities. In Japan, training and career development are like a double helix: continuous and revolving around one another. The Japanese don't have business schools.

115

Frequently, however, their promising managers are sent to American business schools to "learn how the enemy thinks". Multiskilling demands intensive training, because the teams on the shop floor switch tasks between their members as circumstances dictate. The routine of individual workers therefore varies from day to day. Equally, if participative management is to work whereby decisions are pushed down to the lowest possible level, employees must be trained to accept the added responsibilities. Quality control is vital these days in terms of attracting and keeping customers. Yet where a separate department has been set up to administer this function, the initiative quickly peters out. Training alone can make the monitoring of quality second nature to the entire workforce so that audits are unnecessary.

To put training in perspective, there is no way that one sends a semitrained athletic team to the Olympic Games or pits a semitrained national cricket or rugby side against other countries in international tests. One chooses the best and drills them continuously. Business is no different. It is just as competitive. It needs a highly trained team. Moreover, behind the team – as in any sport – should lie a wealth of history and legendary heroes. The most effective team is like a family. One of the reasons many mergers between successful companies fail is the impossibility of combining distinctive corporate cultures which have taken years to evolve.

Another feature that is common to a "winning nation" and a "winning company" is "small government". In a company this means a lean head office: lean in numbers, lean in cost and lean in bureaucracy. If you want highly motivated employees, let them decide how the job can be done better in their own areas of competence. Empower them with training, give them autonomy but then hold them accountable for their results. So many of the previous generation of American textbooks on management sound like Marxist tracts when they urge managers in a heavy-handed way to "plan, lead, organise and control". With their emphasis on a systematic approach to business and memorisable mantras like the one just quoted, they squeeze out the human touch. "Big government" is as lethal to creativity in a business as it is in a nation. Certainly you ought to have: a clear sense of direction and a set of core values provided by top management (the vision); good selection procedures because of the extra trust you're putting in people if you decentralise; information systems that convey bad news quickly so that you can respond fast to correct the situation; and a precise allocation of responsibilities so that each person is in no doubt whatsoever about what he or she is accountable for (and not accountable for, since accountabilities should never be shared). That is good management practice. But don't suffocate the workforce with too many rules, regulations, procedures and forms. Give them wide spaces to roam but make the fences highly visible so that they are aware from a long way off when they're approaching the boundaries of acceptability. If you're a chief executive officer, practise a little MBWA-management by wandering around – to reinforce the values you believe in. And don't ever think you're indispensable – the graveyard is full of people who thought they were!

Wherever possible, departments and workplaces should be converted into profit centres. Nothing gives a sense of purpose better than simple profit-and-loss accounts which regularly measure the financial outcome of each team's efforts. The necessity for fast information systems in big business is underlined by the aggregate $7,6 billion loss made by the big three US car makers in 1991. It only requires slight shifts in revenue and costs – when these figures are huge – for red ink to turn into a mighty river. By making employees themselves aware of the financial state of their microcosm of the business and giving them wider discretion in decision-making, you enable them to take corrective action themselves far quicker than senior management can. Employees' remuneration should include an element of profit-sharing too, thus linking a portion of their pay packets to the company's performance.

No matter how efficient vertical communication is, there's always a time lag as information flows up the echelons of management and decisions come down. Even when the decision arrives, it may not be the best one as the person who made it is probably remote from the problem. Hence, strong lateral communication links between employees on the same level in different departments often eliminate time-wasting loops up and down and improve the quality of many decisions. A "winning company" does not operate like a vertical monolith, but more like a hive of interlocking profit centres co-ordinated from above (the same is true of a "winning conglomerate" except that the profit centres are "focused excellence" operations that have been grown organically). General Motors and IBM, two of the largest companies in the world, are both earnestly converting themselves into highly decentralised operations. The principle that should apply throughout any organisation is that decisions should be made at the lowest possible level. As one American President remarked: "If someone else can do it, I shouldn't."

"Winning companies" have the edge in technological innovation, because they view the process in a different light to the normal linear conception of innovation being the daughter of applied research and the granddaughter of fundamental research. They see innovation in reality as being a much more random activity, where people have sudden flashes of brilliance in which they perceive the profitable conjunction of a new need with a new technology. A perfect example of how innovations happen to link in with one another comes from the British Industrial Revolution. The demand for cheap and plentiful textiles led to a series of breakthroughs: John Kay's flying shuttle in 1733 to improve weaving, James Hargreaves's spinning-jenny in 1764 to improve spinning, Richard Arkwright's water frame in 1769 and Samuel Crompton's mule in 1779 to improve the combined process. Parallel to this, James Watt in 1769 was repairing an atmospheric steam engine patented by Thomas Newcomen in 1705 for pumping water from the mines. He discovered that adding an exterior condenser eliminated much of the loss of power. Edmund Cartwright in 1785 put the Kay-Hargreaves-Arkwright-Crompton advances together with Watt's and devised the first power loom. George Stephenson took Watt's invention further and constructed the first steam locomotive in 1814. So the steam engine, which started out as an invention to pump water, was redesigned to power machinery to manufacture textiles and redesigned again to provide a mechanical conveyance for people and goods. The point is that nobody could have thought through this sequence of discoveries beforehand. Fast-forwarding to modern times, who would have thought before the Walkman came into being that millions of people wanted to walk around listening to music? Sony did and concurrently they saw the technical possibility of miniaturising the tapedeck. Scientific knowledge is useful but it does not in itself lead to innovations. Indeed, a large number of inventions were discovered empiri-

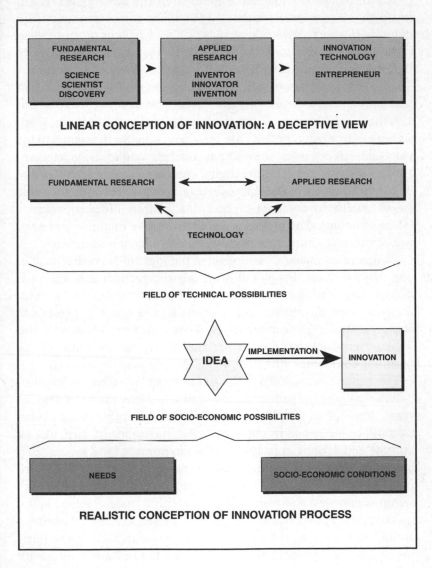

Chart 51

cally before the scientific basis for the invention was fully understood. Metal-alloying preceded metallurgy and the steam engine preceded thermodynamics.

The kind of people that make up research and development teams are therefore very special in that they combine commercial and technological instincts. Even then, only one in a million or more ideas turns into a blockbuster like a Walkman. "Winning companies" give their research teams the breadth of space I was referring to earlier. They don't worry about failures because out of a sequence of failures may – with a stroke of luck – come the next big success. But somehow the "big ones" are becoming harder to discover. Consumer electronics companies are busy searching for the sequel to the video cassette recorder, the compact disc player and the video camcorder. Perhaps it will be the digital compact cassette recorder due to be launched by Matsushita which plays cassettes with the same sound quality as compact discs. In an entirely different industry Glaxo is hoping that Imigran, a drug to relieve migraine sufferers, will be the next Zantac, the best-selling anti-ulcer prescription.

"Winning companies" also reverse the logic of feasibility studies into new products. Instead of designing the product first and then determining a price on which an appropriate return can be earned, they start with the market and calculate a price that the market will accept, given the close alternatives. They then work backwards and design a product that the market can afford. In the minds of the "winning companies" the customer is the centre of the universe.

Two other aspects of the "rules of the game" are relevant for companies that wish to gain or retain winning status over the next 20 years. The shift in people's values indicates that increasingly a business will be judged on its ethics as well as its profits. In particular its attitude and actions in relation to the environment will be carefully monitored. Customers are already using their shopping trolleys to push for a better world. They are buying goods with a "green" stamp of approval and from companies with a "green" image in the marketplace. However, the idea that a new subject called "business ethics" should be added to the training curriculum, as some business schools are suggesting, is to be resisted. The laws of ethics are self-evident. Moreover, like the laws of mathematics, they are universally true: there isn't a special set you have to learn for business (these remarks do not apply to an environmental code that does have to be written down and communicated). In keeping with the more balanced approach to life that individuals are seeking, companies will also be judged on the way they balance the interests of their various stakeholders. Many difficult questions are already being asked such as how much of the total value that an organisation adds to society should be set aside in salaries and wages, how much passed on as dividends to the shareholders, how much reserved for future investment in the business and how much earmarked for social responsibility programmes? Business will have to formulate satisfactory answers.

The final implication for business flowing from the four rules can be drawn from the possible income growth of developing countries in the years ahead. Demographics indicate that the vast majority of young consumers will be living outside the Triad as we enter the 21st Century (the "global teenagers" of Peter Schwartz in his book *The Art of the Long View*). If their disposable income is rising by 5 to 10 per cent per annum, sheer numbers will make them the most important youth market. Thus, under our "High Road" scenario "winning companies" of the Triad will be those which use every opportunity to pioneer new markets in the developing world, rather than those which confine themselves to satisfying the demands of the "rich old millions".

# 2. One "Key Variable"

Having dealt with the four "rules of the game", we must now examine the forces which could drive the world down different paths over the next 20 years. Three areas of major uncertainty have been identified: geopolitical, geonomic (world economic) and societal. Although not shown as such in the diagram, the areas overlap in influence, as reflected in the way we speak of the "political economy" and "socio-political" and "socio-economic" factors. Each area has a pair of outcomes which we shall combine into one "key variable" described in more detail towards the end of this chapter.

### *Geopolitical Uncertainties*

The geopolitical environment familiar for more than 40 years has completely altered with the collapse of communism in Eastern Europe and the Soviet Union, and the dissolution of the Soviet Union itself. These events have promoted stabilising and destabilising forces simultaneously; hence "order" or "disorder" has been selected as the key uncertainty in the geopolitical arena.

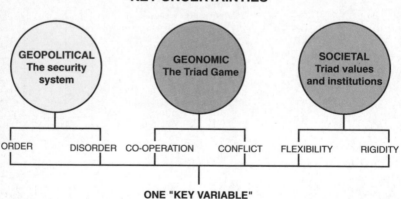

Chart 52

The principal stabilising force of the New World Order, as the post-Cold War period we're in has been named, is the absence of superpower rivalry. Although Russia still has the nuclear capability to level all major US cities in half a day, and will still have it even when each side has cut its ballistic missiles to 3 000-3 500 by the year 2003, for the time being the rulers of Russia are fully occupied with reshaping their own economy. Moreover, the ideological victory of the West is complete in that Russia now subscribes to all the basic axioms of Western governments – pluralism, democracy and the market economy. The Russian doll arrangement – whereby the smallest but most powerful doll was the Politburo, which in turn was covered by the KGB, then the military, then the nomenklatura, then the Party – has been dismantled. The republics of the former Soviet Union have been effectively decommunised with the removal of the dreaded singularity of power which resided in the Kremlin. "Singularity" is a suitable term to use as it also describes the centre of a black hole in space where the gravitational field approaches

## SIZE OF RUSSIA RELATIVE TO OTHER REPUBLICS

*Chart 53*

123

infinite proportions and crushes anything which has the misfortune to fall into the black hole.

Continued reductions in Nato and Russian nuclear stockpiles and in conventional forces are to be expected, lowering the defence burden of the countries concerned and the risks of conflict. The end of superpower confrontation will also curtail their proxy battles in the Third World: corrupt regimes and dubious liberation movements

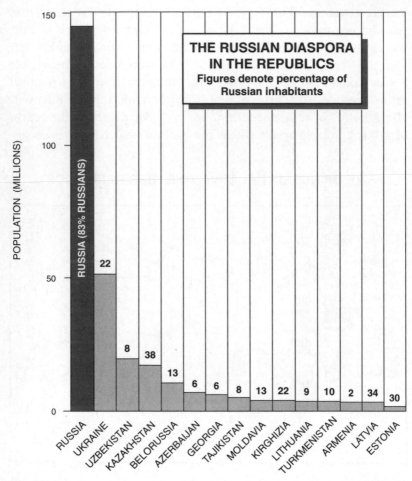

Chart 54

will no longer receive moral or financial support because they're an ally of one or the other. Russia anyway cannot afford it.

At the same time the break-up of the Soviet Empire has opened a Pandora's box of dangerous conflicts stemming from deep-seated national and religious rivalries intensified by economic collapse. Many of these conflicts will take decades to resolve. It is one thing to dismantle the KGB and the bureaucratic apparatus of the past, it is

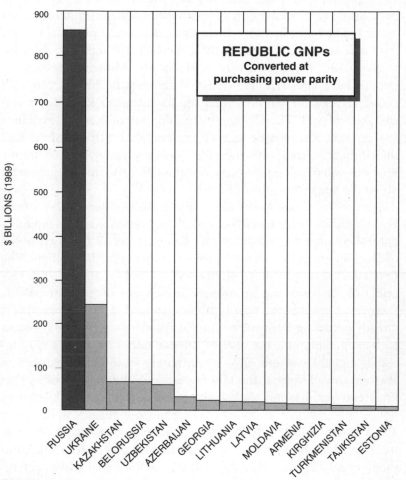

**REPUBLIC GNPs**
**Converted at**
**purchasing power parity**

*Chart 55*

another to build democracy and institutionalise freedom. The second stage requires great perseverance and effort. Meanwhile, society at any time could deconstruct spontaneously into chaos and then relapse into dictatorship.

Will the new club, the Commonwealth of Independent States (CIS), evolve into a worthwhile institution conferring economic benefits on its members and thereby stabilising the former Soviet Union? Russia dominates the CIS through sheer size: demographically, geographically and economically. Russia produces around 80 per cent by value of the CIS's commodities which earn foreign currencies. The range includes oil and gas, diamonds, precious metals, base metals, coal and potash. So if the CIS develops into a "common market" it will be a very lopsided one. Moreover, several republics have already made policy statements hostile to intra-CIS trade: Uzbekistan will no longer sell its cotton to Russia, nor Kazakhstan its gold. The Ukraine by its adoption of currency vouchers and its intention to issue its own currency has introduced another impediment to trade. It's therefore too early to say how economic relations will develop between the republics, or to make a judgment about the longevity of the CIS.

Two other critical issues have arisen: the division of the former Soviet defence force into CIS-controlled strategic forces and republic-controlled other forces; and the treatment in non-Russian republics of Russian minorities which in total number some 26 million. The first issue has bogged down on the definition of "strategic". The second issue is becoming prominent on account of the nationalistic rhetoric of some of the host republics. Indeed, a Russian exodus is already occurring from some Central Asian states. Should Moscow seek to champion the interests of Russian minorities, the level of instability could rise quickly. For instance, in the circumstance of Russian threats against the Ukraine it would be most unlikely that unilateral renunciation of nuclear weapons would remain Ukrainian policy. The incipient problem of the Crimea highlights both issues. The Crimea has a largely Russian population (67 per cent) but was transferred to the Ukraine by Nikita Khrushchev in 1954 to commemorate 300 years of Russian-Ukrainian unity. Its Russian inhabitants voted to stay with the Ukraine in the December 1991 referen-

126

dum, but not by a large margin. Another referendum has been called for, and if it goes ahead the result could go the other way. A complicating factor is the return of tens of thousands of Tatars who are staking a claim to the land they controlled until 1783. The Crimea is also central to the defence issue as Sevastopol is the base of the Black Sea fleet. The fleet is said to contain some 45 large warships, 300 small ships, 28 submarines and 151 planes, but some of the vessels may already have been sold as scrap. Moscow appears to have dropped its claim that the fleet is a "strategic" force. It would also seem that Russia and the Ukraine have agreed to joint command of the fleet until 1995 (whereafter it will be split up) and to joint use of port facilities. Nevertheless, the issue could become prominent again if relations between the two countries deteriorate.

Conditions within Russia itself are highly uncertain. The cautious moves towards establishing a foreign exchange market and full convertibility of the rouble are to be welcomed. So is the fashioning of the loan accords between the IMF, G7 and Russia in terms of which loans may be provided to stabilise the rouble and strengthen the reform process in exchange for good economic management. However, it is not clear how far Russia can meet the stipulations laid down for granting the loans. A good start is that the Russian government appears to have reduced its budget deficit from 20 per cent of Gross National Product in 1991 to 5 per cent in the first half of 1992. On the other hand, Russia is saddled with the bulk of the foreign debt of the former Soviet Union which is estimated to be $60 billion. As regards inflation, freeing domestic prices without imposing monetary control has led to consumers facing price rises up to several hundred per cent. The situation is exacerbated by a monopolistic production and distribution system, illustrated by the fact that in the former Soviet Union three-quarters of the 6 000 most common industrial products were produced in single establishments. Moreover, the one price that has not been liberated as yet is the all-important oil price. It stands at about one-fifth of the world price. Oil is the intermediate input into many products, with the result that, until its price increases to a realistic level, the overall pricing structure will remain distorted. Russia's privatisation plan which involves the issue of vouchers to all citizens to purchase shares in state-owned businesses constitutes the greatest sale ever of state assets. It is a gigantic step in the right direction, if successfully implemented. But like all schemes of such massive dimensions, it is cumbersome and flawed. Meanwhile, little of note has been auctioned so far and the ex-command economy continues to function through inertia. The ensuing hardship is eroding Boris Yeltsin's popularity and may pave the way for unpredictable political developments, possibly involving military malcontents.

Many outcomes are possible for the CIS and Russia. The optimal one would be an Eastern Economic Community with the nomenklatura transforming itself into a business class as the samurai did in Meiji Japan. The greatest obstacle standing in the way of this scenario is the inclination of the nomenklatura to use the transition to a free enterprise system to "get rich quick" – a case of old snouts in a new trough. This will be highly resented by the population at large who will then equate capitalism with a licence to be corrupt. Wrongly, they might pine for a return to the old ways (which were less explicitly corrupt) instead of demanding laws to eliminate corruption in the new dispensation. The most negative outcome would be another Imperial Russian Empire in which the still largely intact military machine would be used to "protect" Russian minorities in the republics. The irony is that the most positive event in our lifetime – the collapse of communism – has the greatest potential for destabilising the world community, not least because of the sizeable nuclear arsenal still around with doubts about whose finger is on the button.

Eastern Europe is less of a threat to the future stability of the region. East Germany is already part of a unified Germany, and Hungary and Poland are both anxious – for political and economic motives – to associate themselves with and ultimately gain membership of the European Community. The situation in Czechoslovakia is uncertain due to the pending separation of the Czech and Slovak nations, but it is probable that a future Czech government will continue to auction state-owned companies to the public. Nevertheless, the short-sighted behaviour of certain West European countries in wishing to retain duties and quotas on many industrial and agricultural imports from Eastern Europe could be a major bone of contention. Moreover, the lower half of Eastern Europe is still (in 1992)

128

in a thoroughly volatile state. Croatia, Slovenia, the rest of Yugoslavia, Rumania, Bulgaria and Albania all have a long way to go before stabilising as free market democracies. Strife there could create a substantial diaspora of poverty-stricken refugees into Austria, Italy, Greece and Turkey. Italy has already had a foretaste with Albanians arriving by boat at its eastern ports.

Moving south, events in the Middle East can have wide-ranging repercussions because of the world's reliance on oil from the region, the close links between the US and Israel and the significant arms build-up yet again following the Gulf War. Peace talks between Israel, Arab countries and the Palestinians have up to now achieved little progress on the central issue of a homeland for Palestinians. However, the election of Yitzhak Rabin as prime minister of Israel signifies a change in sentiment which could open up new peace initiatives. These could very quickly be overturned by a serious terrorist incident escalating into war. On the positive side, any future war could be contained through joint action by America and Russia. Against that the odds of a nuclear exchange are increasing as the knowledge of producing ballistic missiles and nuclear warheads disseminates through the Third World (the nuclear risk also applies to any conflict between Pakistan and India over disputed territory on their borders).

The growth of fundamentalist Islam poses a serious challenge to Western lifestyles and values. This in itself is not a geopolitical problem. It only becomes one if attempts are made by zealots to impose Islam on countries wishing to pursue other paths of development. The attractions to the "poor young billions" of a religion based on the strict code of the Koran are obvious. It anchors their existence in spiritual certainties when all is flux around them; it gives a clear sense of purpose in a world that for many has no meaning whatsoever; and it abhors materialism, a quality the poor do not possess anyway through force of circumstance. The Middle East, Pakistan, the southern republics of the former Soviet Union and northern Africa are all falling under the spell of fundamentalist Islam. That is a formidable area of influence. How much further it will spread and at what rate is unknown. Equally unknown is whether the spreading of an idea will degenerate into a war of beliefs. A nuclear *jihad* is not out of the question. Fundamentalist Islam is a wild card with the ability to alter the balance of power in important parts of the world.

With over one-fifth of the world's population, the future trajectory

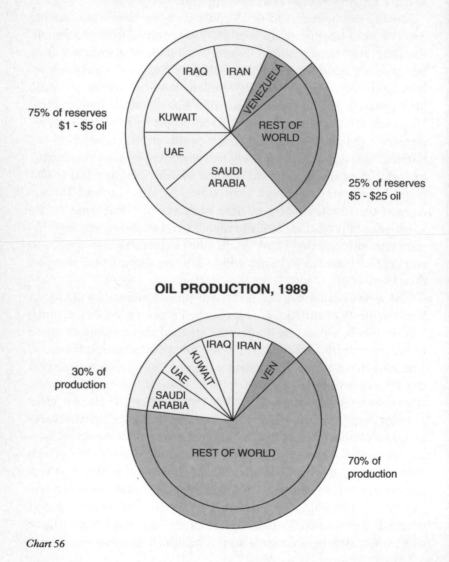

**DISTRIBUTION OF OIL RESERVES, 1990**

75% of reserves
$1 - $5 oil

IRAQ   IRAN   VENEZUELA

KUWAIT   REST OF WORLD

UAE

SAUDI ARABIA

25% of reserves
$5 - $25 oil

**OIL PRODUCTION, 1989**

30% of production

IRAQ   IRAN

KUWAIT   UAE   VEN

SAUDI ARABIA

REST OF WORLD

70% of production

*Chart 56*

130

of China has to be of geopolitical significance. Will the sleeping giant awaken in fitful bouts of rage (more Tiananmen Squares) or rise peacefully to become the largest dragon of all by the middle of the 21st Century (think of a country with more than one billion Taiwanese)? When the present gerontocracy passes away, the next generation of rulers has the choice: replace the communist one-party system with Western-style democracy, or retain the status quo. The only point to be made with some certainty is that the more prosperous the Chinese economy becomes, the more pressure there'll be to liberalise the political structures there as well. At the moment the big three consumer items in China are a colour television, a refrigerator and gold jewellery. The next demand could be more difficult to handle: regional autonomy. At that point, like its crockery namesake, the country could shatter into small pieces without adroit leadership and a safe pair of hands. In other words, China could become another United States of America or cease to exist, like the Soviet Union.

The final geopolitical uncertainty revolves around the kind of geopolitical threat the "poor young billions" in general can constitute to Triad security. It probably won't materialise in a military form because the weapons currently in the hands of the "poor young billions" are no match for the Triad armoury – witness the Gulf War. Of course the situation would change dramatically if the parts to construct a nuclear bomb together with scientists capable of doing it were undetected by the Triad – smuggled into a country with a crazy dictator. Be that as it may, the most likely form for the threat to take is one against which advanced weapons systems and military prowess are irrelevant: it arises from the Triad's encirclement by an outer ring of extremely poor people and an inner ring of gateways into two members of the Triad (Japan has no entry points as it is a group of islands).

Earlier on I commented on the sinister links of drugs, crime and terrorism between the "rich old millions" and the "poor young billions". These have already shown a potential for undermining the social fabric of the developed countries. Drugs, in particular, have probably done more harm to American society in terms of broken lives, crime and loss of productivity than any military confrontation.

131

China was immobilised by opium in the 19th Century; it managed to reduce the traffic only through almost unbelievably harsh measures against those involved in the trade. America would never resort to the same tactics, such as shooting guilty narcotics dealers. The alternative of legalising drugs has been suggested. This would remove the criminal element from the trade but some experts estimate that the consumption of drugs would triple, only worsening the problem. Education in schools on the dangers of drug abuse, as well as alcohol abuse, is probably the best answer.

## THREATS TO THE TRIAD:
## REFUGEES, MAFIAS AND THE UNDERCLASS

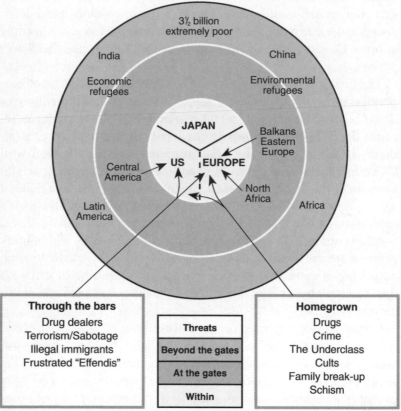

*Chart 57*

The link of immigration, however, could prove to be the strongest geopolitical threat posed by the "poor young billions" to the Triad. In a world of "separate development", where the income gap between the rich and the poor nations widens, waves upon waves of immigrants may arrive at the gates of the Triad – by land and by sea. How will Triadians react as their gates are shaken and sometimes trampled down by the "poor defenceless victims of poverty", only seeking a better life? The answer, if current experience is anything to go by, is stronger bars and tougher padlocks and forcible repatriation of those who manage to slip through the bars. Confusion and chaos would reign as civilised consciences were repelled by pictures of brutal rejection in the newspapers and on the television screens. The full fury of the "liberal establishment" would be vented on the unfortunate watchmen at the gates who would respond that they were only carrying out their duties. Perhaps Americans are having a taste of things to come in having to respond to the herculean efforts of Haitians to reach the US mainland in their frail crafts. At the moment, they are being turned back.

In such a world of "separate development" the Triad would find it difficult to deal with the sullen, unco-operative and for the most part openly hostile governments beyond the gates. Moreover, to assume that those governments would have any leverage over their citizenry would be dangerous. Racked by instability themselves, the poor countries would descend towards anarchy, their impotent rulers unable to deliver on agreements with the Triad on immigration even should they wish to do so.

*Geonomic Uncertainties*

The foremost geonomic uncertainty, at least for the 1990s if not for the opening decade of the next century, is the relationship between the United States, Japan and Western Europe (the Triad game). The three regional economies are roughly equal in size and are engaged in head-on competition at a time when increased co-operation on a range of issues affecting the security of this planet is imperative. Each region has its champions and detractors producing strings of statistics to prove that one or the other will be the ultimate winner – as in any sport. The implosion of the Evil Empire, as the

Soviet Union was once called in the West, has only served to intensify the economic struggle. Neither Europe nor Japan is willing to acquiesce to US demands for changes in economic policy. Likewise, the US does not feel that it has to pamper its allies any more to keep them on side against the Soviet Union. Given the scope for increased economic friction, are we facing a prolonged period of Triad discord? Or will Triad harmony be preserved? Signs point in both directions.

Let's deal with the negative possibilities first. Spurred on by the world's economic recession, the protectionist lobbies in all three legs of the Triad are having a field day. The Buy America First movement in the US, the farmers' support groups in Europe and the Japanese politicians and industrialists who advocate that Japan must continue to play by its own rules – their messages are persuasive and the public receptive. The worst manifestations are when you see public figures in America smashing Japanese radios, Japanese politicians divulging crude analyses of "what is wrong with America", and Europeans trying to limit even the local assembly of Japanese cars and using the excuse of "dumping" to impose arbitrary tariffs on imported hi-tech goods such as Japanese copiers. The possibility of Fortress America, Fortress Japan and Fortress Europe each trading within its own Triad region but not with the others is not to be lightly dismissed. Many people think that the Wall Street crash of 1929 triggered the Great Depression of the 1930s. Not so – it was the Smoot-Hawley Act passed in America to protect domestic industry against foreign imports. Thus began the downward spiral of international trade which caused the Depression. If emotion has its way (which it does with half of the world's history) a repeat of the 1930s is a possibility.

The brighter side of the Triad game is encapsulated in the epigram: "A fool learns by his own mistakes, a wise man by the mistakes of others." Surely G7, the executive committee of the Triad, is peopled by sages who won't allow the Depression to happen again? At least the mechanism exists now to debate these issues before things get out of hand. Monetary and fiscal policies are a great deal more sophisticated than they were 60 years ago: the buffers are there to stop the world economy going into free fall. Business is so much more international these days. In the last resort the huge Triad companies will keep the whole show together. Let's hope so. The Kondratieff waves of the last 250 years indicate a depression every 60 years, just time for the present generation to forget what the previous generation learnt. And don't forget how clan loyalty can metamorphose into belligerent nationalism in hard times.

The other geonomic uncertainty is the economic relationship between the Triad and the rest of the world. The Uruguay round of GATT has not yet achieved positive results; it is deadlocked until the European Community agrees to phase out quickly the favourable treatment of European farmers. Fortunately, the door could be opening now that European agricultural ministers have agreed to overhaul the 30-year-old Common Agricultural Policy and reduce subsidies to farmers (for Europe in 1991 these amounted to over $80 billion and for the Triad as a whole $177 billion). As agricultural exports are the one area where developing countries can compete with the industrialised world, it is absolutely essential that the deadlock should be broken. At the moment GATT is just a "general agreement to talk and talk".

A general cautionary word is also appropriate here about clubs such as the European Community. A club by its very nature confers privileges on its members which non-members do not possess. If the purpose of the club is to maintain open trade between its members, non-members must *ipso facto* face some restrictions. It is to be hoped that these can be kept to a minimum. Another potentially explosive issue concerns intellectual patents. Software piracy in the Asian dragons is reaching alarming proportions. Although copyright law is being strengthened, Western countries are keen to have protective mechanisms written into the final version of the new GATT agreement.

### Societal Uncertainties

Societal uncertainties relate to the possible ways in which each of the three Triad societies will react internally to the global challenges facing them. There are plenty of homegrown threats to US and European social stability: the Effendis within, drugs, crime, decadence, multicultural schism, the underclass, inner-city decay and family

135

break-up. The wheel is still in spin on whether the new "puritanical" values and emphasis on a balanced life sweeping the youth in both regions will outweigh these threats. Japan, being a more homogenous society, has so far escaped many of the malign trends of the last three decades. Nevertheless, there are signs that Japanese youth are treading the same path as British and American youth did earlier this century, not being as inclined to work as hard or make as many sacrifices as their parents. It appears that success inevitably softens the drive to succeed in later generations. From the point of view of the world scenarios we are about to depict, the important question is whether or not the Triad has been so weakened by this internal disintegration of society that it is too weak to help the rest of the world. Do its members have the flexibility to break out of the mould of Western decline in order to lead the world on to the "High Road"?

The second societal uncertainty concerns the will to maintain global security. There are clear linkages between economic performance, technological competence and military superiority. In the early part of this century, Pax Britannica made way for Pax Americana because Britain was beginning to decline along all three axes. Now weakening economic hegemony in the US will almost certainly affect its capacity to develop new military technology and systems. In some areas the United States is already highly dependent on foreign technology; particularly Japanese semiconductors. Moreover, the US budget deficit has focused attention on cuts in defence expenditure as these are far less unpopular than interfering with entitlements and welfare. American troops in Europe have been reduced from 320 000 before the Gulf War to 220 000 at present. Budgetary stringency and the ending of the Cold War are responsible for this.

So where do we go from here, now that no single nation can preserve the peace of the world? Who is going to function as the global cop to maintain the New World Order? This very much depends on how much the strong isolationist instinct which prevails in American society is allowed to influence its foreign policy. As the world's *primus inter pares*, the United States has to lead the way. Europe's varied responses to the future of the North Atlantic Treaty Organisation, Germany's withdrawal from the current European Fighter Aircraft project and Japan's late offer of assistance in the Gulf War indicate that the other two legs of the Triad are both reluctant at the moment to play a prominent role in providing a general security umbrella for the world.

The answer lies in the United Nations Security Council that acted so decisively in the Gulf crisis. For the first time in decades no veto was cast. However, similarly favourable circumstances for taking joint action may not occur again. Any attempt to use the United Nations umbrella to impose order routinely on Third World countries is unlikely to be acceptable to China or Russia. Equally, if Germany and Japan are expected to share in peace-keeping operations as a matter of course, they will want their enhanced status to be reflected in permanent representation on the Security Council. They will demand a say in defining security issues and responses. All this presupposes that Triadians have the vision to see beyond the priorities of their daily lives within their own countries, and recognise that only collective will and collective action will ensure world peace by deterring rogue countries from undertaking military escapades and responding with overwhelming force if they do. The natural response, however, from people leading a comfortable life is to retire into a gilded cage and cling rigidly to the philosophy of not getting involved in other people's problems until it is too late.

The third and final societal uncertainty concerns the harmonisation of values within the Triad itself. What is needed is some convergence in the deeply held values and the long-standing institutions which represent those values in the three regions. Without some degree of unity, the Triad will not be able to provide sufficient impetus to the world economy for the steep climb up the "High Road".

The Structural Impediments Initiative (SII), launched by President Bush and Prime Minister Uno in July 1989 on behalf of America and Japan respectively, is an important start to the process of harmonisation. The stated purpose is to identify and resolve the structural problems which represent obstacles to trade, and to achieve a greater equilibrium in balance of payments surpluses and deficits. The SII agreement was finalised in June 1990. In effect the Japanese have agreed to start playing by the same rules as everyone else, particularly by opening up their market to imports and foreign investment, while the Americans are acknowledging the need to copy the excellent features of the Japanese system. For the first time an international agreement places constraints on the governments in both countries in areas hitherto considered purely domestic domains. Nevertheless it is a bilateral agreement. Europe has yet to come to the party.

Finally, and by no means least, the evolution of values in developing countries is critical to the future trajectory of the world economy; it takes two to tango. It's no good for the Triad to make constructive overtures to the "poor young billions" if their rulers make every effort to stymie these initiatives. The Effendis must be on side too. In other words, the philosophy of free enterprise and small government needs to be embedded in Third World society: there has to be a widespread desire to apply the formula described earlier for becoming a "winning nation". Fortunately, with the demise of Marxism the ground is by and large fertile in most developing countries for ideas favourable to high economic growth to take root.

## One "Key Variable"

The mechanical combination of geopolitical, geonomic and societal uncertainties in every possible permutation gives us eight possible scenarios. Such a number could lead to confusion, not least because there would be little difference between some of the scenarios. But the whole process can be simplified if we assume that there can be only one positive scenario while all the other seven are negative. This is not an unreasonable assumption if we regard a favourable state in each area as a necessary but not a sufficient condition for a positive outcome. It is only when there is a conjunction of favourable states in all three areas that a positive scenario can materialise.

Hence our "High Road" requires a combination of order in the geopolitical sphere, co-operation in the geonomic sphere and flexibility in the societal sphere. Nobody should doubt that it is an extremely tough road to take. Disorder in the world, economic conflict between Triad members or rigidity in values in either developed or

## ONE "KEY VARIABLE"

**Will the Triad foster a sufficiently viable relationship with the developing world so that the "Poor Young Billions" uplift themselves or not?**

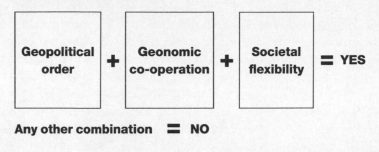

| Geopolitical order | **+** | Geonomic co-operation | **+** | Societal flexibility | **= YES** |

**Any other combination = NO**

*Chart 58*

developing nations is quite sufficient to condemn the world to a long-term decline along the "Low Road".

According to this logic the various uncertainties examined in this chapter can all be merged into the simple question: "Will the Triad foster a sufficiently viable relationship with the developing world so that the 'poor young billions' uplift themselves, or not?" That is the "key variable", which in recent times has become ever more "key" as we classify the former Soviet Union among the "poor young billions".

Using a historical analogy, will the Triad display the same generosity of spirit that the United States showed to West Germany and Japan after the Second World War? Will the developing countries have the same strength of will that West Germany and Japan had to follow the same path to economic success? Only time will tell.

A reader with a competitive instinct might baulk at this uncalled-for charity. The whole point of winning, he or she might declare, is that you beat your opponents. They lose. So why help them, particularly if they're going to end up breathing down your neck (and dragon breath can be very hot)? The answer is that to compete you need an arena. In the context of trade that means a stable world. Having too

139

many losers will destroy the stability of the world. If an elephant ignores the quicksand, the quicksand swallows the elephant. A gentler, more ethical answer would be that life is a mixture of opposites: the yin of winning, the yang of making others winners too.

# 3. The Two Scenarios:
## "High Road" or "Low Road"?

With the one "key variable" mentioned at the end of the last chapter we can generate two scenarios over the next 20 years. If the relationship between the Triad and the "poor young billions" prospers, then an optimistic scenario we call the "High Road" may come to pass. However, if the relationship is negative or non-existent the world will head down the "Low Road".

## The "High Road"

Let's start with the "High Road". Under it, countries within the Triad will grow economically at a respectable 3 to 5 per cent per annum, occasionally registering even higher numbers. Obviously, a cyclical pattern will be superimposed on the underlying growth rate, but never so severely during the 20 years that we will experience another world-wide recession as big as we have now. Rather it temporarily dampens the rate of increase in the Triad's Gross National Product. Developing countries on the other hand average between 5 and 10 per cent per annum economic growth for sustained periods. Rising income per head is no longer the exception but the rule among the "poor young billions". This automatically brings down their higher population growth rates as rising affluence decreases family size. The world population does stabilise in the middle-to-later part of the next century.

This isn't a scenario, I can hear some readers thinking to themselves, this is a pipedream. Not so – here are five reasons why the "High Road" is a plausible option for the world over the next 20 years. Firstly, nearly all poor countries are potentially rich, but badly governed. Remove with good government the barriers to economic growth and the natural work ethic and ingenuity of mankind will do the rest. In China, hundreds of millions of peasants responded to the death of Maoism by working an agricultural miracle, creating an

**A FAVOURABLE WIND FOR THE "HIGH ROAD"**

* Most poor countries potentially rich
* "Dragonology" spreading among Effendis
* New technologies appearing which are easily transferable
* Doubling time in income per head of a "winning nation" shortening
* Economies can grow extremely fast from a low base

*Chart 59*

economic growth rate close to 10 per cent per annum. As poor countries are one by one "dragonised", Triad companies will seek them out as new markets and new export bases before their labour becomes too expensive.

Values favourable for economic growth are ricocheting around the world. The Effendis are learning about "dragonology". They want to be successful, so they're dropping the tired old concepts of Marx and Lenin. Many developing countries are starting with a big plus: they have nothing. That sounds like a contradiction, but think about Germany and Japan. They have gone from being military losers to economic winners. Why did they do that? It's because they had the right attitude after the Second World War. If you have to go back to zero, you take nothing for granted.

We're in the middle of a major technological wave of microelectronics, biotechnology, ceramics, new materials, superconductivity, etc. None of these technologies has been fully exploited yet, and this improves the chances of a prolonged upswing. These days technologies are easily transferable and so can benefit everyone.

The doubling time for real income per head for successful countries in the world has fallen dramatically. It took Britain 60 years after 1760 to double its real income per head. It took the US 40 years after 1840 to do the same. It took South Korea only 11 years to double its income per head after 1966. And with modern technology one could shorten that doubling time even more.

142

Developing countries by their very nature start from a low economic base. You can easily let your economy grow fast from a low base, sometimes extremely fast. Italy achieved a record economic growth of almost 30 per cent per annum between 1945 and 1948. Japan managed approximately 10 per cent growth for 27 consecutive years from 1946 to 1973. Taiwan has been close to that figure for 40 years since 1950, South Korea for 30 years since 1960 and China and Botswana for 10 years since 1980. Each country achieved its spectacular growth rate in its own way. Some are short-term traders, others long-term thinkers (in Japan Matsushita has a 250-year strategic plan). South Koreans tend to congregate in large, export-oriented manufacturing complexes, while Taiwanese prefer the independence of small, also export-oriented, manager-owned businesses. All these approaches work. But there was one common theme: the citizens of these "winning nations" had the will, the self-confidence and the freedom to succeed.

### Eight Requirements

We have eight requirements for our "High Road" scenario. The first is that the Triad shares its ideas and technology with the developing world, rather than its money. If you think back, the US became a great industrial nation on the back of British ideas. Japan used American ideas. South Korea uses Japanese ideas. It's much better to teach a man to fish and equip him with a fishing rod than give him fish. This kind of assistance requires more commitment, time and energy than handing out aid, but the payoff in the longer term is immeasurably higher.

Where money is forthcoming it should come from eager investors. Let developing countries compete for the capital of the world, because by so doing the "poor young billions" will end up being better governed. There's no substitute for good, solid equity investment where the foreign company behind it has weighed up the risk against the return and come to a favourable decision. Chevron has done just that by signing an agreement with the Kazakhstan authorities to develop jointly the Tengiz oilfield at a cost of $20 billion over the next 40 years. The best thing that can happen to any developing country is the conversion of the Effendis there into a new class of entrepreneurs.

**EIGHT REQUIREMENTS FOR THE "HIGH ROAD"**

* Triad shares ideas and technology with developing world rather than money
* Poor countries should compete for equity capital available in the world
* Money should only be lent by world bodies to countries dedicated to becoming "winning nations"
* Pure aid restricted to real hardship
* Equality of opportunity in international trade
* Sound international monetary system
* Arms trade strictly controlled
* Balance of economic development against environmental health

*Chart 60*

The rich countries, the IMF and the World Bank ought to lend monies only to countries clearly dedicated to becoming "winning nations". Certainly where a country is spending a disproportionate amount of its Gross National Product on manufacturing and importing arms, loans should be denied. At the moment the Central Asian/Far East region is importing 35 per cent of the world's arms, more than any other region. If loans are withheld it should be made very clear to the citizens of that country that this action is linked to disapproval of the existing government's policies. That way the people will have an incentive to replace the incumbent rulers with ones more dedicated to the philosophy of the "High Road".

Pure aid needs to be restricted to real catastrophes like earthquakes, floods and famine and – in special cases – to the provision of infrastructure such as hospitals, schools and housing and the protection of the environment. Where possible, international aid should be given direct to the organisation undertaking the relief work or managing the project. It thereby bypasses the sticky fingers of officialdom. Currently overseas aid ranges from 0,2 per cent of Gross

Domestic Product for Ireland and the United States to a high of just more than one per cent for Norway.

There has to be genuine equality of opportunity in international trade, in other words a level playing field. It means that the Triad eliminates its barriers against imports from the Third World, particularly agricultural goods and textiles as these are the two things the Third World can provide competitively to the First World. At the moment, for example, the World Bank estimates that the Multi-Fibre Arrangement entails lost earnings of $75 billion a year for developing countries because of bars on their textile exports. The Triad also stops dumping its own highly subsidised agricultural surpluses on others around the globe.

A sound international monetary system allows a sufficient expansion of liquidity to underpin the expansion of trade that will follow any lowering of barriers. It is estimated that the elimination of all restrictions on trade could add more than $250 billion to the world's Gross National Product of $20 trillion.

The arms trade, especially the movement of ballistic missiles, chemical weapons, biological weapons and nuclear devices must be very strictly controlled. Where possible, the weapons should be destroyed. More teeth and money are given to the International Atomic Energy Agency to vet any initiative made by any country in the nuclear field. In order to contain aggression and end wars that break out, the United Nations, backed up by G7, becomes the world's policeman and peacemaker. The Triad picks up most of the tab associated with the expanded role of the United Nations. This assignment is going to be very tough in light of the fragmentation of the world into smaller nations and may require the expansion of permanent membership on the Security Council to give it extra clout.

Finally, we know that it is not worth having an economic boom followed by an environmental bust. We have to balance economic development against environmental health. Again the United Nations and G7 are going to have to take some very tough decisions about the environment and then make them stick. Where pollution laws are broken the polluter should pay dearly.

In the short term, probably the most important implication of the "High Road" scenario is that Russia, the other former republics of the Soviet Union and Eastern Europe have a chance to stabilise their societies and build up democratic structures. The climate is favourable for the green shoots of free enterprise, that are just beginning to appear, to flower into respectable businesses competing in the world marketplace. A positive sign is that the young Russian Effendis who have joined Boris Yeltsin's team have totally absorbed the capitalist paradigm. In their 30s and 40s, they are the new revolutionaries intent on overturning the communist paradigm of their geriatric predecessors.

## The "Low Road"

We have, on the other hand, the option of the "Low Road" for the world over the next 20 years. Unlike the "High Road", where favourable conditions on all three fronts – geopolitical, geonomic and societal – are demanded simultaneously to get there, we have multiple entry points for descent down the "Low Road". General chaos in the world, Triad discord as the regions fall out with one another, Triad weakness as its members' societies disintegrate because of

---

**"LOW ROAD"**

* "Rich Old Millions" retire into "gilded cage"
* Outside the cage billions of poor clamour to be let in. Only elite permitted
* Restrictions on international travel
* Eastern Europe and ex-Soviet Republics collapse
* Chaos elsewhere with Mafias, death squads and a thriving security industry
* Triad uses hand-outs, but hand-outs don't work
* UN becomes "Tower of Babel"
* Environment destroyed by poverty

---

*Chart 61*

crime, drugs, decadence, schism or other social ills brought on by a low economic growth rate – any of these is sufficient to trigger a "Low Road" scenario. In addition one must not rule out a return to the Cold War, or even a switch to a hot one, should Russia's present rulers be replaced by a military regime pledging to restore the country's former glory.

### The Gilded Cage

Nevertheless, the most probable entry point to the "Low Road" is where the Triad collectively turns its back on the rest of the world. It retires into its gilded cage. If you talk to the average American, the average European and the average Japanese, they're not really that interested in the rest of the world. They have their own lives to lead, their own priorities to schedule. They elect governments that are going to look after their interests within their own countries. They filter out the sufferings of the world. To reach out to the "poor young billions" therefore needs a special kind of vision and enlightened self-interest, qualities that many Triadians do not possess. So for us it's that third option which really could occur.

Outside the gilded cage, billions of poverty-stricken people struggle to survive as the globe deteriorates into a crazy quilt of clans. The Triad maintains physical clamps on immigration and economic clamps on trade. Only the elite from the developing world are welcomed through the bars of the cage, thus stripping the developing world of the very people they need. However, millions of other unskilled people pitch up unannounced at the borders of the Triad. Since goods can't move because of protectionism, people do.

The "rich old millions" steer clear of tourism outside the Triad because they worry about winding up as hostages to the "poor young billions". Or it may simply be the fear of being mugged in the megacities that puts them off. For Triad travellers, therefore, the planet shrinks. For Triad diplomats who are posted to the Third World, training in self-survival is part of their career development. Triad embassies become impenetrable forts.

Eastern Europe, Russia and the other republics collapse. Migration becomes a general evacuation. The number of people leaving the Soviet Union – 39 000 in 1987, 453 000 in 1990 – swells to a million a year. The mountain of business debt, which is building up through lack of cash, triggers a chain reaction of bankruptcies, unsound businesses dragging down those which are sound. The Russian health system sinks into an abyss: even now half the rural hospitals and clinics have no sewerage connections, 80 per cent have no hot water and all suffer from a lack of rudimentary equipment such as disposable needles and sterilisation units. The infant mortality rate, already high at 33 per 1 000 live births compared to 5 for Japan and 8 for Britain, rises even further. Miserable and cold, the hungry bear begins to prowl. The worst outcome is that Russia and the Ukraine fall out over the Crimea or some other issue. An old African expression says that when two elephants fight, the grass gets hurt as well. A conflict between these two countries, with such massive firepower on both sides, would have severe repercussions for Europe.

Chaos and disorder reign elsewhere in the world, upsetting the movement of base metals, oil and other commodities. Mafias thrive, crime soars, left-wing guerillas fight right-wing death squads, security guards multiply, and the poor become criminals of necessity. To show how low the "Low Road" can go, in one Colombian city the well-to-do not only have high walls around their houses and bars on their windows, they also have steel girders above their gardens to stop their children being abducted while playing outside. Colombia has a million security guards in a population of 30 million people.

The Triad intervenes only if its security is threatened, as in the Gulf. Tension builds up between the Triad and China as Beijing refuses to stop its secret trafficking in nuclear technology to Third World countries. Meanwhile, China continues with underground testing of nuclear weapons.

The "rich old millions" use hand-outs to try to placate the rest of the world. Europe bales out Russia, the US bales out South America, and Japan bales out Cambodia, Vietnam and Laos. But, as we all know, hand-outs don't work in the long run because they reward failure and create a dependency culture. A global redistribution of income will merely make matters worse.

The United Nations becomes a Tower of Babel with bitter altercations between the rich and the poor countries. The Triad is perceived as using its position on the Security Council to impose minority rule on the world. The "poor young billions" demand that the United Nations be run on the more democratic basis of one person, one vote. For example, Chine represents 1,1 billion votes, the United States 240 million.

Finally, we witness ecologocial destruction on a scale never witnessed before as desperate people cut down trees and overgraze the land in order to survive. So our "Low Road" is a very grim prospect.

## The Crossroads

The world is at the crossroads. We are the first generation that can irreversibly transform this planet for the worse; we are the last generation that can avert disaster. We are not at the end of history, as some people believe; we are at the beginning of a new chapter.

Think back to the Romans. When the Romans started out they

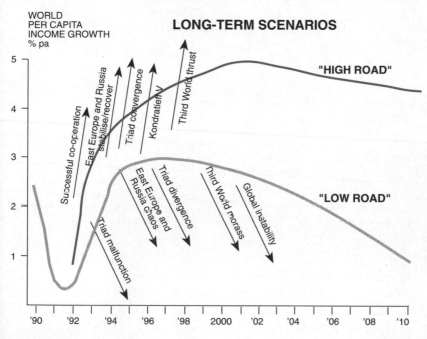

*Chart 62*

had low walls and wide openings, so that if an enemy attacked them they counter-attacked fast; they wer keen young warriors. They ended up with high walls and narrow gates, because they were frightened old men. And the end was inevitable. Rome was sacked by the Goths in AD 410. The moral of this story is that if the Triad does not go to the Third World, the Third World most assuredly will come to the Triad.

We have gwo kinds of future: the active future that you make happen, and the passive future which you let happen to you. the "High Road" is about the active future, in which the Triad assists in turning the "poor young billions" of this world into heroes and champions. Like the incoming tide, the Triad lifts all the boats – belonging to rich and poor alike – at the same time. The Triad does something extraordinary, something which goes beyond the normal motivations in a "business as usual" scenario. For the "High Road" is possible: otherwise the "Low Road" is inevitable.

# 4. South Africa:
## Microcosm of the World

*Applicability of Global Presentation*

Much of the content of our world scenarios must sound very familiar to South Africans. Indeed, we have generalised, to cover the world as a whole, the original "High Road" and "Low Road" scenarios we wrote in the early 1980s specifically for South Africa. How can this be? The answer is that South Africa is a perfect microcosm of the world: the challenges facing South Africans to create a better society are identical to those facing the Triad and the developing nations.

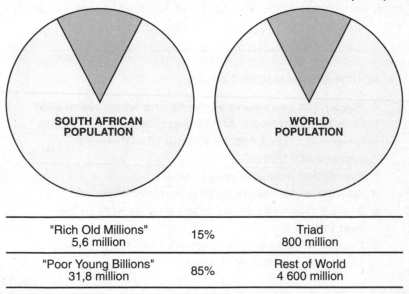

**SOUTH AFRICA AS A MICROCOSM OF THE WORLD (1992)**

SOUTH AFRICAN POPULATION

WORLD POPULATION

| | | |
|---|---|---|
| "Rich Old Millions" 5,6 million | 15% | Triad 800 million |
| "Poor Young Billions" 31,8 million | 85% | Rest of World 4 600 million |

*Chart 63*

151

*Population*

Let's go through each section of the global presentation to see how it applies to the South African situation. We start with the first "rule of the game": population. During the 1980s South Africa's population grew at 2,5 per cent per annum, well in excess of the average economic growth rate of 1,5 per cent. Like most developing countries, South Africa was poorer in terms of per capita income in 1990 than it was in 1980. We are in the poverty trap here, but how is that poverty spread? The breakdown between "rich old millions" and "poor young billions" in South Africa is 15:85, exactly the same ratio as for the world. South Africa's population was estimated to be 35 million in 1990 and is expected to rise to 47 million in the year 2000, an annual increase of 1,2 million.

Only 13,5 per cent of South Africa is classified as arable land (crops can grow on it without irrigation) whereas 86,5 per cent is non-arable because rainfall is too low, the slope is too steep, the land is reserved for urban usage, industry or roads, etc. Population pressure and over-intensive cultivation are already taking their toll on rural areas. South Africa's greatest export is topsoil, flushed into the rivers and ultimately the sea at a rate of 300 million tons a year. The

---

**SOUTH AFRICAN POPULATION**

 * **Population increasing at nearly one "Namibia" a year**
 * **Only 13,5% of South Africa is arable land. Per capita water run-off is 1 500 m³ compared with world average of 7 000 m³**
 * **Population pressure now critical**
 * **Informal settlements need a permanent home**
 * **Some 4 million South Africans may be HIV+ in the year 2000**
 * **Critical window of two years when Aids education could make all the difference**

---

*Chart 64*

Karoo is spreading eastwards at an alarming rate because it is 30 per cent overstocked with animals. Emissions in the eastern Transvaal Highveld total 125 million tons a year. The combined annual run-off of South Africa's rivers is calculated to be 1 500 cubic metres per capita compared with a world-wide average of 7 000. Not only are we running short of water, we have a mismatch in distribution. About 42 per cent of the country's urban population live in the Pretoria-Witwatersrand-Vereeniging complex but the rivers of the Vaal River catchment area provide a mere 8 per cent of the total run-off. Natal's gold is the water the Transvaal so desperately needs.

To add almost another Namibia every year to the country's population when the environment is deteriorating at the rate it is, and the most critical of resources – water – is already spread so thinly across the nation, is nothing short of committing ecological suicide. Just as we all live in one world, there is only one South Africa. The "rich old millions" and the "poor young billions" here have to develop a constructive relationship in order for the country as a whole to survive. And the choice for the "rich old millions" is precisely the one that faces the Triad: to reach out and help the "poor young billions" uplift themselves or to retire into a gilded cage by building higher walls, buying a couple of Rottweilers and a pistol, and installing more sophisticated security systems. Which is it to be? I hope that the recent experience of informal settlements being moved from pillar to post as each middle-class residential community cold-shoulders them is not an indication of future relationships. "Nimby-ism" (not in my backyard) is merely the local equivalent of the gilded cage. Even if a political settlement is shortly achieved, the next 20 years is critical in terms of reducing population growth. The surest way of doing this is to target an economic growth rate approaching 10 per cent per annum and bring the "poor young billions" into the economic mainstream so that the benefits are felt throughout the entire spectrum of society.

Two other points about the Triad are relevant to South Africa. Firstly, since Triad markets represent some 80 per cent of the world's income, any South African company with ambitions of becoming "world class" must have a subsidiary, associate or just a presence of some kind in each leg of the Triad. We must be close to the customer too. Secondly, because Triad companies venturing outside their home base have tended to invest in other Triad countries for reasons of security, South Africa will need to use all its powers of persuasion to attract them to come here. Sub-Saharan Africa is particularly badly placed if the US, Europe and Japan set a priority of looking after the "poor young billions" in their vicinity first.

## Aids

At the moment the proportion of South Africa's total population infected by the HIV virus is estimated to be below one per cent. Nonetheless, the latest projections for the country in the year 2000 are that between 3,7 and 4,1 million people could be infected with the HIV virus, giving a seroprevalence level of approximately 8 per cent. In that year nearly 260 000 people could be ill with full-blown Aids. We are at a moment in the evolution of the disease in South Africa when small changes in behaviour can have a particularly powerful effect on HIV spread. It is therefore not predetermined that the figures quoted of HIV infection in 2000 will be reached. South Africa probably has a two- to three-year window to mount an effective Aids-prevention campaign in primary and secondary schools and among the adult population at large. If Aids does hit South Africa hard, it will above all be a tragedy to see so many lives prematurely ended. But it will also cause tremendous economic dislocation and place a severe burden on our health system. And by creating a plague mentality it may interfere in the process of reconciliation that South Africa so desperately needs in the coming years.

## Technology

The current technological wave of microelectronics has the same implications for South Africa as for the rest of the world: a radical restructuring of labour patterns. Big business, in a direct sense, will only be able to create a fraction of the employment opportunities needed to absorb new entrants to the labour market as well as those currently unemployed. Major plants being built now, by incorporating the latest advances in automation and process control, will require workforces of hundreds and more rarely one or two thousand. However, there is an important multiplier effect which must not be

154

## SOUTH AFRICAN TECHNOLOGY

* Big Business has important "multiplier effect" for employment but microelectronics will restrict direct jobs
* Microbusiness development essential to solve unemployment plus ladder to go to the top
* Good image of quality and service vital for South African industry overseas
* "Biotech" offers many opportunities for South African agriculture
* "Affordable" technology to protect the environment

*Chart 65*

overlooked. During the construction phase, contractors and sub-contractors will be utilised and the disposable income of their employees will generate additional economic activity. Furthermore, once the plant is commissioned jobs will be created in companies supplying the plant with goods and services.

The argument sometimes put forward that in a country like South Africa, where job creation is so desperate, big business should voluntarily decline to use state-of-the-art technology in favour of labour-intensive processes, ignores commercial reality. I have yet to come across any customers demanding goods in a shop that have been labour-intensively assembled ahead of those that have not. It's the best quality at the best price that counts: the customer is king. Any large company that sub-optimises on production processes for the sake of extra jobs will immediately lose out to local competitors, and certainly won't be able to take on the Triad giants in the export field. An exception is whether a company has a nonracial employment policy: this may influence a customer's decision.

The only conclusion, therefore, is that the alleviation of unemployment here – or anywhere in the world – necessitates a highly focused governmental policy on the promotion of small business and microenterprise. The removal of bureaucratic hindrances to the establishment of these businesses must be the first objective. This should be backed up by a ladder of institutions that supply key functions to a business as it progresses from the scale of micro to the scale of macro. Key functions include the provision of finance and commercial training. South Africa already possesses several private institutions servicing entrepreneurs on the bottom rung of the ladder. They're doing outstanding work, administering stokvels, running "township MBA" courses, etc. The higher rungs of the ladder where single employee businesses become multiple employee businesses are not so firmly established. Ultimately the ladder should reach into the formal sector by incorporating institutions such as the Stock Exchange and the commercial banks. What one is looking for is a visible path that any aspiring young entrepreneur can take to evolve his or her business into one of the future giants of South African industry. Some will make it to the top, some will stop at lower levels of the ascent because they don't want to go higher, and others will go bust. That's life. If you examine the history of many of the successful multinationals, you will see that they started out as a one-person show: but that person had an extraordinary degree of vision and vitality.

Microelectronics has one other important message for South African companies: to add real value to your product you have to give it a strong personal orientation. The word "commodity" not only applies now to wheat, cotton, steel, copper, etc, it also covers basic appliances like televisions and video cassette recorders. A company can earn a reasonable profit margin on sales of such goods only if it has developed a strong brand image: something that puts its products above the many alternatives available on the market. With the return of South Africa to the world fold, it's vital that the country's businesses create a widespread image of reliability, quality and after-sales service among overseas customers. It took Japan 30 years to transform its image from supplier of copycat, down-market radios, cars and cameras to pace-setter for excellence and originality in these categories. South Africa has a golden opportunity to establish first-rate credentials from the word "go" because its long absence from many markets means that the ground is completely fresh.

Biotechnology, the next wave, could have far-reaching conse-

156

quences for South Africa. We are very lucky to have one of the best biotech units in the Southern Hemisphere in the Microbiology Department at the University of Cape Town. At present, in collaboration with the South African Sugar Association, they are working on injecting genes into bacteria so that they mass-produce a toxin against the Eldana borer, the scourge of Natal sugar cane. If the experiments are successful, original sugar cuttings will be dunked into bacterial fluid and thereby rendered automatically toxic to this insect, and pesticides will no longer be required. Frost-resistant plants, virus-resistant maize, fruit and vegetables that stay fresh for longer – biotechnology can do so much for this country's farming community.

Equally, technology can rescue South Africa's environment but it must be affordable. We cannot adopt Europe's standards here if by so doing we divert a disproportionate amount of the country's capital resources away from economic development. The dilemma of Eskom provides a neat example. The primary target of Eskom over the next decade must be to electrify every single township in this country. Not only will this cut out the dreadful pollution caused by coal-burning stoves, it will reduce the cost of energy to township residents. Moreover, residents will be able to use the whole gamut of modern household appliances. Microbusiness will also be stimulated. The cheapest way to satisfy the objective of universal electrification of residential areas is to build another coal-burning power station close to the coal seams in the Eastern Transvaal. If the new power station is like the existing ones, it will add to the sulphur dioxide emissions which are already considered perilously high, not least because the Eastern Transvaal Highveld has one of the world's worst dispersal climatologies. So what does one do? Try to save on electricity elsewhere is one answer, so that the spare capacity can be utilised by the townships. This can only be temporary, since economic growth – especially under a "High Road" scenario – will increase demand for electricity to the extent that the current grid is no longer capable of supplying it. Whichever way one looks at it, another power station will eventually be needed.

At this point the environmental lobby in any Triad country would suggest equipping all the power stations with desulphurisation plants. These do not come cheap. In fact, for a single 3 600 megawatt station the capital cost of adding such a plant is somewhere between R500 million and R1 billion and the running cost over R100 million a year. To write this off, Eskom would certainly have to raise the price of electricity, hitting the poor as well as the rich and raising the general cost structure of industry. The trade-off in South Africa's case between the economic and social upside of providing cheap electricity and the environmental downside of doing so is very different from the position that would pertain anywhere in the Triad. The solution here is to go ahead with construction of a new coal-burning power station when it is required, using whatever technology to lower emissions is available at the time and lies within the constraints of South Africa's financial resources. Combined cycle gas turbine technology may point the way. At the moment, Eskom is installing at two of its power stations new bag filters which are highly effective at collecting ash. Technological advances in Australia to increase the lifespan of the bags from less than a year to $4^1/_2$ years have brought the cost of such measures within Eskom's ambit.

The same line of argument should be used when examining how to lower pollution caused by traffic in South African cities. The Californian option of insisting on zero and ultra-low emission in new cars is not practicable here. We probably ought to rehabilitate and extend our mass transit systems – again in a way that is affordable.

### Social Values

In regard to the two aspects of mankind which have never changed, namely the desire to kill and the desire for roots, South Africa is no different. The first aspect is sadly reflected in the daily death toll and mounting cases of violent crime one reads about in the newspapers. For many, national issues are irrelevant as their lives are governed by armed gangsters. Their communities have been Sicilian-ised, not democratised. Mafia-like terror haunts their every move. To overcome this horrible trend necessitates a multifaceted strategy.

The community needs to be totally confident that the police are not only on their side but will protect them with as much force as is needed to quell crime. Only then will people feel brave enough to break the omertà (conspiracy of silence) and turn the criminals in.

## SOUTH AFRICAN SOCIAL VALUES

* "Sicilianisation" of townships. Gun control vital, but "nothing stops the bullets like a job"
* To hold together, South Africa must be a club worth belonging to
* Government of national unity a way of bringing people together during transition, but South Africa should move to multiparty democracy as soon as possible
* Focus on community for a million little "melting pots"
* "Dragonology" now accepted in South Africa, but "Effendis" use it wrongly to justify socialism.
* Balance between economic development, environmental health and quality of life will be a uniquely South African one. No models to follow

*Chart 66*

Gun control has to be thoroughly applied and the sources of illegal arms identified and charged. In the US the TEC-9, a machine pistol manufactured in Miami, is the weapon of choice among gangsters. Here it is the ubiquitous AK47 – the Soviet Union's only "successful" manufactured export. This firearm is responsible today for more violent deaths of people (and wildlife) in Africa than any other modern or traditional weapon.

To decriminalise society also requires massive job creation. As one American priest said: "Nothing stops the bullets like a job." A job comes before a house (think of all the ghost towns in areas where industries have declined or mines have closed down) but jobs do not come before customers. Somebody out there must want something that the market is not supplying, or is supplying at too high a price for a job opportunity to exist. The entrepreneur is a vital catalyst in the job creating process because he or she is the one who matches demand with supply. The reason why so many government initia-

159

tives to create jobs fail is because the market has not been correctly assessed by someone with an entrepreneurial flair. Nevertheless, the construction of houses and schools provides obvious candidates for some kind of community service programme where the youth of South Africa is universally given a chance to learn basic job skills. To succeed, it must not be undertaken on a nationwide basis, nor should it be seen as a paternal gesture to losers. Rather the programme ought to be community-driven and yield tangible results for the participants which, apart from a modest financial reward, should include a vote of thanks from the community for the projects when completed. Unless something drastic is done to curtail crime, we will follow the United States pattern of African American middle-class families moving as quickly as they can out of "poor young billion" residential areas to "rich old million" suburbs for a quieter life. The crime bosses left behind become the models of authority for the youths to follow. The latter form a "kid-ocracy" under which any attempts to re-establish parental control are treated with contempt.

As to the desire for roots and the inclination of people to break up into clans, South Africa – like any other nation-state that wants to hold itself together – has to evolve into a club to which everyone wishes to belong. If force is used to retain members it will lead to civil war. The association needs to be voluntary and desired. Hence no constitution will be worth the paper it's written on if it doesn't carry the support of the principal parties. While we all know that minority rule of majorities is anti-democratic and wrong, recent evidence from around the world suggests that minorities do not lie down meekly under majority rule if they feel the dice are loaded against them. Hence the need for a Bill of Rights to protect individual liberties, and an independent judiciary to enforce it. From a different perspective, no constitution will last long unless the common man and woman living under it perceive that they have received direct economic benefits from its existence. An unusual clause that could be put into a constitution would restrict government spending to 30 per cent of Gross National Product. From that one condition, everything from a balanced state budget to low inflation and high economic growth flows.

To counterbalance the clannishness that exists in South Africa

160

will require powerful all-South African symbols. Sport is a manifest way of bringing everybody together under one banner. Many people would also suggest the adoption of a single official language, but language is such a touchy area that it is best left to natural evolution as to whether one language dominates over others. The recent dissension over flags and anthems reveals how difficult the task of unification is going to be when so little of symbolic significance is shared from the past.

In the short term the most potent way of beginning the process of substituting the all-embracing "we" for "we-they" is to have a government of national unity articulating a common vision for the country – inspiring people to drop their clan loyalties in favour of a broad commitment to make South Africa a "winning nation". It is "us" versus the rest of the world! A unity government would also soothe nerves and serve as a neutral backdrop to an elected constituent assembly while it formulates a new constitution. However, there are some cautionary points. Firstly, the manner in which a unity government is established is crucial since any hint of co-option will tarnish the reputation of the participating individuals within the ranks of their own supporters. Secondly, it should be a brief episode, its sole purpose being to act as a bridge between the Old and the New South Africa. A unity government is after all the antithesis of a properly functioning multiparty democracy where the electorate has a choice and governments have the potential to change. The sooner South Africa can, within practical bounds, complete the transition to a fully-fledged democracy the better. Hong Kong is a good example of how the uncertainty of a drawn-out transition can adversely affect a community's prospects (and they must wait till 1997). Finally, the vote is a fundamental form of self-expression. Until it is exercised, people will seek to assert their existence through less conventional means.

Seeking a common vision is probably more effective at lower levels of society where bonds are more tangible. For example, if people vow to each other that they are not going to let down their community, their company or their sports team through internal division, the camaraderie generated can subdue all clannish feelings. Schools that decide to integrate can do the same for children. A million little

161

"melting pots" like this would go a long way to healing the wounds of apartheid. Ultimately the most powerful glue is success.

In terms of the shift in global values, the debate in South Africa has also been affected. No longer are the Soviet Union, China and Cuba glorified by the left-wing Effendis as exemplary economies to copy. They do not want their credibility eroded by being seen to back losers. So they've chosen the Asian dragons as the new models for government intervention. They are "socialist" successes. Now this is arrant nonsense because "dragonology" accepts as its starting premise that business and the profit motive are central to a viable society. Any intervention by government is therefore wholeheartedly supportive of the private sector. Socialism, on the contrary, is about top-down state control of the commanding heights of the economy, in other words regulating and restricting business for the nobler cause of creating a better society. Business is an incidental liability to be carefully monitored, not an essential asset to be enthusiastically fostered. Beware, therefore, of turncoat South African Effendis preaching a new gospel, or overseas Effendis who regard South Africa as the last place on Earth to sell their outmoded ideas. They will swear that their revamped model of socialism is the one that will succeed, whereas all the others failed for extraneous reasons. Theirs is the brilliant breakthrough! But the world has moved on.

One can find no better place for the principle of a balanced approach to life involving economic development, environmental health and quality of life to be applied than the sensitive issue of future land ownership in South Africa. As a first priority it must be a goal of this country to possess a thriving, competent agricultural industry. This entails shunning the course that the former Soviet Union and other developing countries adopted of turning their farming sectors into ideological playgrounds. The consequence of such actions is clear from any visit to these countries: barren land, broken-down tractors, a precipitous fall in agricultural output and the switch from net food exporter to reliance on international food aid.

As a second priority, the environment has to be respected. In South Africa this means that fragile areas like the Karoo and the rest of the non-arable pasture land must be farmed as large units in order

162

not to put too much pressure on the ecology. Smallholdings are just not possible on this type of farmland. The vision that the country can be wholly converted into a patchwork of small peasant farms will very quickly become the nightmare of desertification as it has done in large parts of the homelands.

But we have the third priority of improving the quality of life of all the citizens of South Africa and, specifically, redressing the injustices of the past where land was confiscated from black farmers.

So where do we go from here? No magic formula can be offered: it is going to need a hard-headed analysis of what is practical within all the constraints listed above.

*"Winning Nation"*

The six unchanging characteristics of a "winning nation" ought to be seared into South Africa's consciousness if we are to go head-to-head with the Asian dragons.

Nobody anywhere can deny the principle of equality of oppor-

---

**SOUTH AFRICAN EDUCATION**

* **Pre-primary and primary schooling should receive top priority**
* **Streaming at secondary level with emphasis for many on practical skills training, but no downgrading of best schools**
* **Tertiary education should be flexible, e.g. students at technikons can switch to university and take their credits and vice versa**
* **Literacy training a community initiative**
* **More bias towards mathematics and science**
* **Devolve more authority to schools themselves**
* **Potential for computer-aided education**

---

*Chart 67*

163

tunity, particularly when applied to children starting out in the world. The focus of any future South African educational policy has to be first and foremost on pre-primary and primary education. That is the equivalent to the foundations of a home: secondary education is the walls and tertiary education the roof. Without sound foundations, a house will fall. It is essential that as soon as possible South Africa reaches a position of universal pre-primary and primary education of an acceptable standard. Virtually every other function of state should be subsidiary to this one, so that the best brains and the necessary funds can be applied to the fulfilment of this objective.

It took Japan 75 years to progress from the goal of universal compulsory primary education set in 1870 to an equivalent goal in secondary education established after the Second World War. Obviously, South Africa has to do better than that. After primary school, children can be streamed into high schools, technical colleges and other institutions offering a combination of academic courses and practical skills training. At the secondary level, the worst policy would be to go the British route (until recently) of trying to make all the schools the same, i.e. comprehensives. To downgrade consciously the best schools in the country in the interest of banning elitism is educational madness. It takes decades – if not a century or two – to build up the ethos and traditions of an outstanding educational establishment. Tough entrance exams may be required to preserve equality of opportunity. Moreover, the network of scholarships and bursaries will need to be enhanced to cover the fees of children from deprived backgrounds. By all means build new schools which one day will compete with the best in the land, but don't do away with the priceless educational assets that the country already possesses – it would be like clearing an age-old indigenous forest.

As with secondary education, tertiary education can come in many forms: universities, technikons, specialised colleges, apprenticeships, on-the-job training and for those who missed out on decent schooling, literacy programmes. I can see some readers quibbling with such a wide definition of "tertiary", but it is important to realise that education continues for life and the educational system must cater for people of all ages coming in and out of it as and when they personally want to enhance their knowledge and skills. The University of South Africa among other exceptional institutions represents the modern approach to education: to make a limited core of academic excellence available on as wide a basis as possible to people of every conceivable background and age. Flexibility for students to switch from universities to technikons and vice versa and carry their credits wherever they go will be a further step towards optimising the educational process.

Literacy training has to be a community initiative. Churches and the existing network of charitable organisations such as Rotary clubs are the kind of channels which can be used most effectively for spreading the word. Any company worth its salt should have a literacy programme for employees desiring to advance themselves in the organisation. A brilliant programme I've come across uses the well-known national advertising slogans and names of products to teach literacy. Appropriately it is called Brand Knew.

One feature of the Japanese and South Korean education systems we should copy is the bias towards science, mathematics and technology. Japan produces 500 engineering graduates per million citizens: South Africa produces 30. South Korea produces 20 technicians per science graduate: South Africa produces 0,8 i.e. we have more graduates than technicians! There has been a tendency in this country to put non-scientific qualifications on a higher plane than engineering, chemistry, physics, etc. Perhaps this snobbery was an unfortunate inheritance from the British academic tradition that rated Latin and Greek the purest of all forms of knowledge (hence the term "Greats" for a classics degree at Oxford).

Universities should become centres of excellence with close ties to industry. Given the critical shortage of top-class researchers in South Africa, it makes sense for the relevant departments at universities to spread their skills between basic and applied research: universities will also have a better idea of what to teach their students to prepare them for the world of business afterwards. Industry on its side must continue to provide financial assistance to universities in order to retain the world-class expertise that might otherwise depart for greener pastures.

165

Devolution of authority to the schools themselves to choose their own teaching methods within a national curriculum is much to be desired. No one, least of all the Effendis, has the answer about what is the best way to teach children. Let every school experiment, and through a process of comparison and cross-referencing the superior approaches will become known.

Lastly on education, I believe there is enormous potential in using computers, videos and other hi-tech equipment to assist in the classroom. Technology will not instantly convert bad teachers into good teachers nor will it substitute for the human touch in the classroom. But technology will certainly make good teachers go further (and improve the skills of inexperienced teachers through training). Every child should have access to the best teachers in the land and some of the ones overseas. If those teachers can't be there physically, the next best thing is to have them on the screen. Why not videotape their lessons and pass them around the country so that we mass-merchandise knowledge? Why not take one channel of SABC television and roll lessons throughout the day and have the books available in CNA? Then we're starting to get serious about education in this country. Star Schools in Johannesburg has pointed the way with its brilliant screen-based programmes, coincidentally showing how cheap such methods are with a large consumer base. It estimates that 180 days of instruction cost as little as R10 per pupil (you don't pay a video a salary). St Alban's College in Pretoria is pioneering the use of hi-tech systems to raise the educational standards not only of their own pupils but of as many Mamelodi schoolchildren as they can incorporate onto their Statech educational grid. At one pre-primary school in Johannesburg, four-year-olds have their own computer room. Children are amazingly adept at using computers and establish a one-on-one relationship with the screen very quickly. Moreover, because a child cannot be a passive observer with a computer-based programme in that he or she has constantly to key in data and instructions, there's no time to be bored and inactive. Finally, for the real cynics about this form of education, one can only say that it is better than no education at all (which is the case with many youngsters in this country).

The second condition for a "winning nation" is a work ethic.

That South Africa already possesses because the country has never suffered from over-welfarisation. To keep it that way we must refer back to the four prerequisites of a work ethic, the most important being "small government". The greatest risk in the way of South Africa making a successful transition to an open democracy is the substitution of a new ideology for apartheid, with massive government intervention in pursuit of that ideology. The obvious candidate is affirmative action by quotas in the name of reparation for past wrongs. As the saying goes, "Two wrongs never make a right." They don't even get you even. Nobody disputes the principle of equalising opportunities by undertaking major initiatives in education, training and career development and by removing all discriminatory barriers (glass ceilings and walls) to advancement. That type of affirmative action, if indeed the meaning of the term can be stretched to include that sense, is to be roundly supported. But to jump from that to blatant quotas which ignore merit will reinforce the dimension of colour. How do you choose people who qualify to be included in the quota? How do you handle borderline cases? It's the old trap of apartheid. For whatever the answer is, it goes completely against the grain of non-racialism. Furthermore, it will have the undesirable consequence of demotivating not only those excluded from the affirmative action programme but also the many who qualify, but who have genuine merit and do not want others to think that they've got where they have done because of the programme. Specifically, if experience elsewhere is anything to go by, it will lead to a doubling of the civil service as each post is twinned for existing and new incumbents. With this extra baggage, the South Africa bus has insufficient horsepower to negotiate the steep climb onto the "High Road". It will stop or, worse still, roll backwards.

South Africans will have to kick the habit of "looking to Pretoria" as the nanny who will cure all economic and social ills. Big government is endemic in the South African psyche. This is not surprising when so many people work in state or parastatal institutions, and 90 per cent of media coverage is on what politicians are doing and saying to one another. The "High Road" is about substituting self-reliance for the centrist paradigm. It's about making the future happen in your own community and not stopping to ask what the

167

people at the centre might say. "Small government" demands a revolution in outlook expressed in the words: "I am determined to do my bit to change the world."

On the second prerequisite for a work ethic – low tax – South Africa is already past the upper limit of the range for a swiftly developing country. Government expenditure is 35 per cent of Gross National Product compared with a desirable ceiling of 30 per cent. The question is therefore how the Budget can be trimmed while at the same time more money is allocated to areas of highest priority like education. It means the ruthless paring of expenses in the less important fields of government activity and the retrenching of superfluous Effendis. Economic growth is like demand: it has an elasticity curve. Steep prices curb demand. Similarly, the higher the tax rate the lower the economic growth. In practice, therefore, total revenues to government can actually fall if taxes are pitched so high that they put a brake on economic activity. Certainly a slightly more modest tax structure plus economic growth of 3 to 5 per cent per annum will provide any new government in South Africa with sufficient revenue to undertake all the upliftment programmes required. Perhaps the best way to cope with any bulge in the government's capital expenditure programme during the transition process is to finance it with the proceeds of privatisation of various state-owned businesses. This approach has certainly worked overseas.

The third prerequisite for a work ethic is a sound family system. That delicate web of familial connections must be repaired thread by thread, because kids learn their values at home. The existing informal settlements around South Africa's major cities have a marvellous social network. These settlements should be upgraded with the necessary water reticulation, electricity grid and sewerage systems. The last thing to do is sweep the shacks away and build tall tenements. They tried that in England and Scotland and it destroyed the social fabric of the communities which moved into the new estates.

Finally, to maintain a work ethic you need clean government. This means government whose actions are transparent to the public and a cabinet where each minister is held accountable for the actions of his or her department. If significant fraud or malpractice is uncovered in that department, the minister resigns. It also entails the establishment of a multiparty democracy so that ministers know that their overall performance is judged on a regular basis through the ballot box. For this reason, although a government of national unity is a good thing to have as a transitional arrangement it is not good for accountability in the longer run. Japan is an apt illustration of how corruption can spread in political circles if one party stays in power for too long. No matter how excellent a constitution is, if the government ruling the country becomes complacent because of lack of a competitive opposition its integrity will go downhill fast. Too many jobs will go to pals, too many Effendis will join the gravy train. One would hope therefore that South Africa will eventually develop a two- or three-party system, each party vying for power and comprising a broad cross-section of South Africans with similar beliefs, rather than confining itself to representing narrow clannish interests. Fortunately, South Africa does not possess a predominant clan like some other African countries. So any party appealing purely to clan loyalties is extremely unlikely to win an election. The field is wide open for building political movements on ideas. An added blessing is that the natural balance of power here implies swings of the pendulum in elections, as and when the "floating vote" changes its mind. Any politician, therefore, who fancies that he can rule this country indefinitely will most probably have his dreams rudely shattered.

To act as a watchdog over the government we need a totally free press. The best way of achieving this objective is to encourage the establishment of as many independently owned television channels and radio stations as the airwaves permit. The print media have no limitation on publications other than demand in the marketplace. Undoubtedly there is safety in numbers. The more sources of information the public has and the wider the spectrum of opinions expressed, the closer it will get to the truth. One has to be suspicious, therefore, of calls for unity (except as a temporary measure in the exceptional circumstances we find ourselves in today). It is important to remember that the basis of a healthy democracy is at least a duality if not a greater variety of viewpoints of how a country should be governed. Just as democracy falters when too much power is con-

169

centrated in one place, it also malfunctions if too much credibility is given to one belief. Democracy thrives on the cut-and-thrust of dialectical argument conducted in a debating chamber under the watchful eye of the public. One of the most precious "yin-yangs" of life is the ability to put forward one's views with total commitment but with an ear cocked for someone expressing a superior opinion.

The third condition for a "winning nation" is a high savings rate. South Africa's current personal savings rate is abysmally low at about 2 per cent of personal income. Even though one must add corporate savings – which are healthy – to personal savings to arrive at the national savings rate, it must be prudent to aim for an increase in personal savings. This will only happen if we can bring inflation down to single figures so that savers obtain a real rate of return on the money they're lending.

So the party's over: the lights are out. The current tough monetary policy of the South African Reserve Bank is absolutely right. Moreover, continuing to award ourselves double-digit salary and wage increases for no increase in productivity (South Africa's productivity has been flat for the last 20 years) is the best way ultimately to send either the rand or our export industries into a tailspin. It would be a pity now that sanctions have been relaxed if South Africa completely priced itself out of world markets through its inability to stem inflation. It took five years from 1984 to 1989 for South Africa to move from the cheapest to the most expensive gold producer in the world. Now our gold mining industry is bearing the brunt of the low gold price.

Another thing that has to stop is government "dissaving", in other words the government borrowing money to finance its current spending as opposed to capital expenditure. In every year since 1984, except 1990, dissaving has taken place. In 1991 it was 2,5 per cent of Gross Domestic Product. Not only is it bad business practice to increase your debt to cover running costs, it diverts savings from where they can be used more productively.

On the investment side we have paid the price for having the economy distorted by high inflation and negative real interest rates making capital appear cheaper than it is. In addition, "strategic" import replacement programmes have made us pour money into sub-

## SOUTH AFRICA'S AVERAGE CAPITAL OUTPUT RATIO

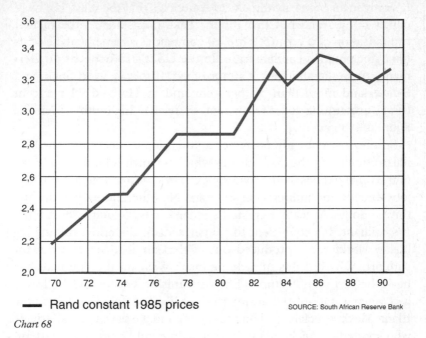

**—** Rand constant 1985 prices

SOURCE: South African Reserve Bank

*Chart 68*

economic projects, while artificial decentralisation policies have encouraged people to invest in the wrong places. South Africa's capital-output ratio, the rands the country invests for a fixed amount of output, has risen steadily since 1970. Put another way, the quality of our investment has declined. Hopefully, with South Africa's return to the world economy we've turned the corner and will invest more efficiently in the future.

The fourth condition for a "winning nation" is a "dual-logic" economy: big business and small business working alongside one another. Strangely, there's a widespread myth in South Africa that somehow big business is bad for the country. But every "winning nation" has its coterie of world-class companies. Volvo in Sweden, Shell in Holland, Nestlé in Switzerland, Boeing in America, Toyota in Japan – these countries regard their giants as major assets to their economy. What's more, the smaller the country's economy the larg-

171

er a world-class company is in relation to the overall business sector. It's only in an economy the size of America's that the really big businesses don't stand out that much. Take one statistic: the market capitalisation of a country's top 10 companies as a percentage of its total stock market capitalisation. In the US it's 15 per cent. In Germany, Australia and Italy it's more than 40 per cent; in Spain and Switzerland more than 50 per cent and in Holland 74 per cent (Shell accounting for 33 per cent by itself). In South Africa the figure is 46 per cent.

South Africa already possesses a "dual-logic" economy, the best illustration being the taxi industry which is worth R4 billion in terms of the value of taxis on the road alone. It has created roughly 300 000 jobs directly and indirectly in six years. No other industry in the history of South Africa has created so many jobs in such a short time. It's brilliant. It's equivalent to 60 per cent of the entire mining industry workforce – produced out of thin air with no government support. Why did this miracle happen? Well, on the one hand we have the taxi manufacturers like Mitsubishi, Toyota and Volkswagen making state-of-the-art microbuses like the Zola Budd and now Elana Meyer specials, and on the other hand we have the taxi drivers who spotted the niche left by the inflexible public transport system. What holds them together isn't philanthropy or charity: it's pure commercial gain. The auto manufacturers make a lot of money out of producing the taxis and the drivers earn their living by driving them. That's the "dual-logic" economy for you.

The Anglo "small business initiative" was established in 1989 on the ground that it was possible for our mines and industrial companies to forge profitable links with small business in this country. And so it has been. Our companies make substantial savings by contracting out some of their work, while the small businesses get the contracts plus a certain amount of guidance from the client on managerial techniques and financial controls. Contracts have covered work like lathing and grinding, timber reclamation from underground, manufacture of steel wedges and overalls, industrial catering and cleaning, and signwriting.

There's plenty of potential for big and small business in South Africa to join hands in a synergistic way, the one creating employment through the multiplier effect and the other generating jobs directly. One request, though, to the urban planners of the future: please come up with sensible urban layouts that permit the first logic economy (shops) and second logic economy (hawkers) to co-exist.

The fifth condition for a "winning nation" is social harmony. South Africa needs this quality almost more than any of the others. Entrepreneurs cannot be creative if they're worried sick for the safety of themselves, their families and their property. Until the violence in South Africa dies down you can forget about Triad companies allocating significant amounts of money to this part of the world. Neither can entrepreneurs, local or foreign, operate in an economy where the sword of Damocles of state intervention or nationalisation hangs over their heads. Uncertainty, either because of violence or because of government policy, is the biggest killer of investment. But, as was quoted earlier, "Nothing stops bullets like a job." Alas, there's a bit of the chicken-and-the-egg here. Peace and prosperity are mutually reinforcing.

The sixth and last condition for a "winning nation" is to be a global player. South Africa because of its gold mining industry has until recently suffered from a misconception which prevails in some countries rich in one or two mineral resources. They wrongly perceive they'll never have to diversify into other industries. So they don't and they decline. Meanwhile other countries, like Japan and Switzerland which do not possess real mineral wealth, are resilient as they've always lived off their wits. Nonetheless, from the mid-1980s and concurrent with the flagging fortunes of gold, South Africa's manufactured exports have soared at a compound growth rate of 12 per cent per annum. We may have escaped being permanently scarred by our mineral wealth!

If South Africa has real ambitions to be a world player, it will have to woo the successful companies overseas to come here. For they have the technical expertise to produce sophisticated consumer goods for local and foreign consumption. They will not come unless restrictions placed on them are virtually non-existent other than the common law of the land. Any high-handedness by a future government will condemn South Africa to the status of a lonely suitor. Furthermore, the idea that government can by decree create thriving export industries is wide of the mark. All one can do is provide an attractive set of export incentives and pray that some able entrepreneurs out there will take the bait.

To judge South Africa's progress towards becoming a "winning nation" a reader may wish to repeat the exercise I did earlier with the Triad and award this country points on a scale of 0 to 1 for each of the six conditions – and review the results once a year.

A lady in an audience once asked me whether "winning nations" remain winners. Distressingly, the answer has often been no because in the season of success are sown the seeds of failure. Complacency sets in and dulls the competitive edge. She then enquired why I wanted South Africa to become a "winning nation" if I knew it would go over the top. My reply was that it is much better to have been a "has-been" than a "never-was" – or a "never-will-be"!

### *"Winning Company"*

Turning to "winning companies", South Africa has its fair share of world-beaters. But it also has its "Head Office Effendis" swelling the budgets and overgoverning the employees. Very few companies here are really lean at the centre. Unreal jobs abound and that must change.

Education and training will have to be the centrepiece of the human resources function in any South African company with "world-class" intentions. Inevitably, overseas (and perhaps many local) customers are going to check whether the recruitment and employment policies of the organisations with which they're doing business stand up to scrutiny. Equality of opportunity and nonracial manning will figure high on their list.

Another area to watch is social responsibility. Anglo has always followed the credo of its founder, Sir Ernest Oppenheimer, who said in 1954: "The aims of this Group have been – and they still remain – to earn profits but to earn them in such a way as to make a real and permanent contribution to the wellbeing of the people and to the development of Southern Africa." This defines the way we do business in the Corporation. The question in future will no longer be whether or not a company should contribute towards the common weal, it will focus on how much time and money should be set aside

174

to do so. In public perception, ethics will count as much as profits.

Within the context of social responsibility falls environmental management. The debate in South Africa on the trade-off between economic development and environmental health is now robust enough for companies in all sectors to know that they ignore the environmental lobby at their peril. While it is necessary to have an environmental code covering each aspect of a business from initial feasibility studies to construction of plants and up to their eventual operation, it is more important to instil an environmental *ethic* in the workforce so that they naturally respect Nature. This dissemination of environmental values can only come from the very top of an organisation.

### Two "Key Variables"

In assessing the possible paths that South Africa can take over the next 20 years and ignoring the impact of wild cards like Aids or a 10-year drought, one arrives at two "key variables" which sequentially follow one another.

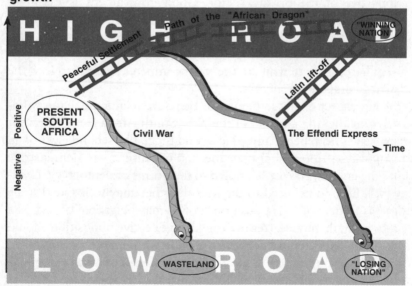

*Chart 69*

175

The first is whether the current process of negotiation will lead to some form of transitional arrangement and ultimately to an acceptable democratic constitution, or whether the parties will break up and declare war on one another. It is well to remember that many matches are won or lost in injury time. The second "key variable" only comes into play should there be a positive outcome to the first variable. It is whether the new government installed under a new constitution will pursue policies favourable or prejudicial to economic growth.

### The "High Road"

There is only one "ladder" which in the near term can lead to the "High Road". South Africa has to reach a peaceful settlement as quickly as possible. Every day wasted in a stalemate is a day spent on the sidelines with other countries increasing their lead on us. Once back in the race, South Africa must take the path of the "African dragon". This is exceedingly tough because it entails the country putting every ounce of energy it's got into becoming a "winning nation". Likewise, the Effendis need to be incorruptible and wholly supportive of the private sector. Good government is essential. However, none of these points preclude the idea that South Africa may have a different party or coalition of parties in power at, say, five-year intervals along the path. The electorate needs to decide on a regular basis as to who are the most competent people to lead the "African dragon" to success.

A key aspect of any settlement is therefore to guarantee that whoever wins the first election of the New South Africa cannot prevent themselves from being judged a second time. The second election in many ways is more vital than the first because it will demonstrate that the country has settled down to the norms of democracy. Leaders will have to get used to the idea that they may well spend some time as leaders of the opposition. Power may be gained or lost by a party more than once. Yet the role of an effective opposition should not be underestimated, for it is the body whose main purpose is to maintain accountability in government circles. A political career will then be as risky and uncertain as that of a scenario planner.

South Africa has four great strengths to help it in its ascent to the

"High Road". Firstly, it has the best infrastructure of any developing country in the world. South Africa's modern network of roads, railways, bridges, electricity, telecommunications, airports and harbours is unrivalled. It's a marvellous launch pad for future economic growth, but we must extend that network throughout all areas of this country, particularly to the disadvantaged communities. I'm especially thinking of electrification. We also have the invisible infrastructure of a banking system, a stock exchange, relative tax stability, commercial law and labour legislation – features for which the Russians would give their eyeteeth.

The second strength we have lies in the abundant mineral resources of this country, as long as we're never complacent again. For the record we're number one in gold – the oldest brand in the world – with 40 per cent of global reserves. We're also number one in chrome (54 per cent of global reserves), number one in platinum (78 per cent of global reserves) and number one in manganese (82 per cent of global reserves). In fact if you take the value of minerals in the ground per head, we're still one of the richest nations in the world despite over 120 years of mining. But what we must now do is go downstream on those mineral resources, add value and turn them into semimanufactured and manufactured products. Look at the difference between Thailand and Australia. Thailand has been the fastest-growing economy in the world because they went downstream into sports goods, jewellery and textiles. Next door you have Australia with a debt of over US$100 billion. It's because they never

---

**SOUTH AFRICA'S FOUR STRENGTHS**

* **Best infrastructure in Developing World**
* **Abundant mineral resources still remaining**
* **"World in one country" could mean tourist Mecca**
* **Nation of entrepreneurs waiting to be released**

*Chart 70*

went downstream on sheep and iron ore. The purchasing power of the Triad companies will ensure that margins on commodities are never too generous.

The third strength we have is the natural beauty of South Africa. We are a world in one country here, possessing 20 300 species of flowering plants, 800 of birds, 243 of mammals, 84 of amphibians and 286 of reptiles. Neither does any other country have its own floral kingdom. We do: it's the sixth one, entitled the Fynbos Kingdom and found in the Cape. With the beauty of the Cape coast, the Drakensberg in Natal, the game parks in the Transvaal and the wide open spaces of the Free State, South Africa could become the principal tourist attraction in the Southern Hemisphere – if it plays its cards right. Indeed, tourism could overtake gold as the country's chief foreign exchange earner as we move into the next century. But we shouldn't invite the lager-sipping English yobbos: they must continue to go to Spain. What we want is the ecologically sensitive tourist.

And the last strength we have is the people of South Africa. We are a nation of entrepreneurs and shopkeepers here – outside the civil service, that is! There is a long tradition from when the first diamonds were found in Kimberley, through the mining magnates at the beginning of this century, to the revolution in small business today. Thousands of small businesses are opening up, now that the economy is being deregulated. The owners come from all walks of life but they're brilliant entrepreneurs, and they are changing the face of the South African economy. Look at Khayelitsha, a township on 3 000 hectares of sand-dunes outside Cape Town. Its annual output of goods and services was recently measured at R74 million. This included taxis, *spazas*, barber shops, small manufacturing operations, cobblers, tailors, etc. Not even the richest farm of an equivalent area in the most fertile region of South Africa has a turnover like that. It's a tribute to the entrepreneurial genius of Khayelitsha that they can produce so much of value from such a barren place – and not a government official in sight! Around 70 per cent of the houses have backyard businesses.

With those four strengths we think it is entirely plausible that South Africa's economy can grow at somewhere between 5 and 10 per cent per annum. It has to, for the chances of a country making a successful transition to a democratic society are low without high economic growth. The current example of the former Soviet Union bears out that proposition. Yet the recession we've had may prove to have been a fitting prelude to our conversion into a dragon. It has shown the politicians how hard it is to make money in business!

One final benefit of the "High Road" could be the creation of a Southern African Common Market. It would make sense for South Africa to import oil from Angola and agricultural produce from Zimbabwe and Mozambique in return for manufactured goods. There's plenty of potential for trade which is mutually beneficial at this end of the continent. If the whole of Southern Africa doesn't prosper, there won't be stability on our borders and refugees will continue to pour in as they are currently doing from Mozambique.

### The "Low Road"

The "Low Road" is where none of these good things happens, because South Africans put a tunnel at the end of the light. The descent to the "Low Road" is represented by two snakes. The first one is possibly only a few throws away: the parties irrevocably terminate the negotiation process or walk out on each other in an interim government. The alternative snake occurs later on after the first universally elected South African government has taken office. Unfortunately the new government applies the wrong economic policies in an attempt to gratify the immediate expectations of the bulk of the electorate.

Let's look at the first snake. The idea that the main players in South Africa could declare war on each other is very frightening. The Yugoslavian civil war demonstrates just how quickly clan warfare can develop into a full-scale, extremely nasty confrontation where no laws of honour apply. If that happened here the consequence would be tyranny and a permanent state of emergency. Ultimately we would all be losers living (and dying) in a wasteland, having provided the international media with acres of interesting coverage while we turn our cities to rubble like Vukovar or Sarajevo. One hopes that at all levels of society the chemistry of negotiation is strong enough and the goodwill around is deep enough for South

179

Africa not to land on this snake and dive into oblivion. The reality is that no party can have it all in this heterogeneous society. The go-it-alone option is a dead end. It would be tragic if a series of outrages sparked an all-out conflict and let the chance of peace slip away for ever. Alas, history reveals such acts of madness come like bolts out of the blue.

If the first snake doesn't bite South Africa, there is another one lurking further down the trail at the point where a newly elected government takes office. It is long, slithery and highly poisonous and has been suitably entitled the Effendi Express. One can hear the station-master yelling: "Roll up, ladies and gentlemen. Climb aboard the Effendi Express to Utopia. All third-class passengers are entitled to travel first-class at no extra charge. If you alight at Redistribution Junction we guarantee there's a house, a car and a job waiting for you together with a bank balance we've managed to extract from those greedy, grasping rich folks. They're not so high and mighty now." It is such a seductive refrain for the "poor young billions". And the Effendis are past masters at making their promises sound genuine. There is no mention that in return for the joyride they offer the Effendis will interfere in every nook and cranny of your life – from your job to your leisure, your sport and the news that you receive. Eventually the public tumble to the fact that it's all lies after years of bloated state bureaucracies, hyperinflation, corruption, emptying shop shelves and generally miserable living conditions. Education and health crumble. The only seriously rich people to emerge from the decline are the Effendis themselves and their wives, living in fortified palaces. However, by then it may be too late because the Effendis are too entrenched (and they put on such a charming front for the media). The end-state is not as dramatic as the wasteland. It's an economy that drearily runs down, an environment that slowly collapses, a country from which the young and able emigrate – a "losing nation" that nobody cares about.

Nonetheless, built into our scenario model is an opportunity to disembark from the Effendi Express. Democracy may hold on just long enough for a second election to take place, sweeping into power a government that promises less and does more. By then a new generation of Effendis may have the right ideas, having experienced the failure of the old ideologies at first hand (you only have to meet a new Polish, Hungarian or Russian Effendi to know exactly what I mean). The second chance to ascend to the "High Road" is described as Latin Lift-off in praise of those Central and South American countries who've recently converted to "dragonology". But no one there will ever forget all those wasted years and the additional time required to become a "winning nation".

### Reasonable Grounds for Optimism

We believe that these paths – two ladders to the "High Road", two snakes to the "Low Road" – are the real options for South Africa. Having said that, our scenario team in Johannesburg is optimistic about South Africa's future for several good reasons. Above all, South Africa has come a long way since 1986 when I first outlined the possibility of a "High Road" for the country. Remember: I gave as the fifth rule for South Africa's political scenarios "But Statutory Apartheid will go." It's gone. We have avoided the snakes at the bottom of the board and climbed a few ladders. If in my presentation then I had listed every single change that has actually taken place during the subsequent six years, nobody would have believed me. A statement therefore that the next six years will see a similar quantum leap of progress is not unreasonable, although it may be greeted with another wave of cynicism.

Despite the horrors of the violence, the rhetorical flourishes from every quarter that pepper the media, the "demands that must be met" and so on, the central logic of negotiation is likely to prevail. The visceral hatreds which stand in the way of settlements elsewhere in the world are not apparent in South Africa. Moreover, the quality of the principal actors on this country's stage is such that they are unlikely to let the future scripting of the play fall into the hands of Effendis of the negative kind. We shall see a reasonable constitution being fashioned out of the principles agreed so far: proportional representation, a two-chamber parliament, a separation of powers between the presidency, the legislature and the judiciary, a Bill of Rights and a sufficient degree of "regionalism" to cope with the country's heterogeneity.

We have other in-built stabilisers: a modern economy where negotiation is entrenched as the principle for resolving conflict within the bounds of what is practical and affordable, a thriving informal sector, a love of sport that unites people, and a whole host of other diverse interests which will provide stiff resistance to any attempt by anyone to monopolise our lives with their politics and ideologies. Finally, the momentous new wave of values sweeping the world – stressing pragmatism over extremism, ethics over ideology – is breaking on our shores too. South Africa could not have chosen a better moment in the world's history to go into transition.

## Turning Ordinary People into Champions

When I was doing the roadshow between 1986 and 1988, with two of my Anglo colleagues, the three of us gave the "High Road" presentation to about 100 000 people on about 500 occasions. We crisscrossed the land, talking to every conceivable community. It was the experience of a lifetime. The first book I wrote, *The World and South Africa in the 1990s*, has now sold 73 000 copies, which is a record for non-fiction in South Africa – though some people call it fiction. In the Welkom CNA it was put under science fiction! And the video of the same title is close to Michael Jackson's *Thriller* at the top of the South African charts of best-sellers ever made. So the ideas of our scenario team have proved far more popular than any one of us originally dreamt would be the case.

I have also talked to some of the leaders of this country. Mr de Klerk and several of the members of the present cabinet heard the talk late in 1986. Mangosuthu Buthelezi and his cabinet heard it in 1987. At the beginning of 1990, I was invited to Cape Town to see Nelson Mandela while he was still in prison, because he had read the book and wanted to discuss the conclusions with me. So the "High Road/Low Road" is in the heads of the leaders of this country as well.

However, what I keep saying to people is that this country is not going to be saved by a black Messiah or a white Messiah: it's going to be saved because we turn ordinary people here into champions.

It is no coincidence that the most successful countries in the

182

world do not have strong leaders in the traditional sense. Go to Switzerland: a handful of people know who their president is, the others don't care. There's not a photograph or statue of him anywhere. It's because Switzerland is one of the richest countries in the world, at $30 000 a head. They ski, they bank and they make watches. Japanese prime ministers come and go, but it doesn't alter Japanese economic growth by a whisker. The reason is that the Japanese prime minister is a facilitator between the major interest groups in Japan, he's not a cult hero.

In Italy they have until recently had one of the fastest-growing economies in Western Europe. Why? Simply because the Italian government is permanently paralysed. So you don't need one great person – a Maggie Thatcher, a Charles de Gaulle, a John F Kennedy or a Winston Churchill – to lead you out of the desert to the promised land: it's not like that at all. The secret is turning ordinary people into champions. Modern leadership is about supporting people, bringing out the best in them, liberating their spirit and making them leaders themselves.

### Middle Class

What one needs for the "High Road" is a strong, productive middle class. The Chinese had one in medieval times and they were the richest nation on earth. In 1900 two of the most successful countries in the world were Australia and Argentina. They had very talented middle classes in those days: unfortunately for them, they have declined ever since. In a recent survey the Japanese were asked: "What class are you?" and 95 per cent said: "We are middle class." So it is the middle class that makes or breaks a nation.

There's an old middle-class saying that I dearly love: "If you need a helping hand, you'll discover it at the end of your arm." But you have to train, develop and educate that arm; you must give it equality of opportunity. You must grant the arm access to the land, the capital and the other resources of the country; you must have equality of access. You must protect the arm with rule of law, and you must heal the arm when it is sick, with adequate medical facilities. But after that it's up to the owner of the arm to make his or her own way in the world.

### Redistribution of Knowledge and Skills

Our "High Road" is about the redistribution of knowledge and skills in the short run, in order to create a permanent redistribution of income and wealth in the longer run. South Africa is not a particularly rich country. Its current income per head is around $2 700 per annum which puts it in the central group of the middle income nations. Confiscating the wealth of the 15 per cent or so "rich old million" South Africans, who have spent years accumulating it, will not particularly help the "poor young billions" but will certainly create a dead or moribund society. You can plunder the many to enrich the few, but you cannot plunder the few to enrich the many. The successful entrepreneurs, who are the engine room of the wealth-creation process, would be highly demotivated by such an act. A far worthier and more effective course is to improve everybody's potential with education, and at the same time eliminate all barriers to the fulfilment of each person's ambition. That way, the sky's the limit for all South Africans.

No wiser words can be found than these to support the point being made here: "You cannot strengthen the weak by weakening the strong. You cannot help the small man by tearing down big men. You cannot help the poor by destroying the rich. You cannot help the wage earner by pulling down the wage payer. You cannot keep out of trouble by spending more than your income. You cannot further the brotherhood of man by inciting class hatreds. You cannot establish security on borrowed money. You cannot build character and courage by taking away a man's initiative and independence. You cannot help men permanently by doing for them what they could and should do for themselves." Who said this? Abraham Lincoln in the middle of the last century.

### Individual Accountability and Individual Initiative

It comes down to individual accountability and individual initiative. This is illustrated by one more story from my visit to Japan. I was standing on Tokyo station with my Japanese host, waiting for a bullet train called the Hikari Super-Express to take us from Tokyo to Osaka. I asked him how often the train was late. He said, in measured terms: "This line has been open for seven years. The cumula-

184

tive lateness of the Hikari Super-Express over those seven years is 120 seconds." Whew, I thought to myself. We got on the train, arrived at Osaka on time, had three days of business there and then went back to the station. At the ticket office there was a sign that surprised me because it said: "All trains cancelled." I turned to my Japanese host and said: "Aha, you see Japan doesn't always work." Do you know what he did? He took out a handkerchief, mopped his brow and said: "It's all my fault." Can you imagine that? "All my fault!"

What had happened was that one of the worst typhoons in 30 years had struck Japan and washed part of the line away, but it was all his fault. In a trice I understood what it was that made Japan such a great nation. It was this deep sense of individual accountability and responsibility. This is what has driven them to produce zero-defect cameras and zero-defect cars for their customers. But they also have this sense of accountability towards the community. I went round a shrine in Kyoto on a Sunday afternoon after thousands of people had passed through that shrine, yet there wasn't a speck of litter on the ground.

Can you imagine anyone in South Africa saying "It's all my fault" – about anything? Here it's the government's fault, society's fault, the system's fault, your enemy's fault: it is never ever your own fault. The buck stops nowhere. It ricochets around like a bullet in a rocky canyon. And as for littering in total disregard of the community – it's terrible. Somehow we are going to have to recapture that feeling of individual accountability in South Africa. Maybe the two most important words to start off the New South Africa are: "I'm sorry."

Turning now to individual initiative, there's an old maxim, "Where there's a will there's a way." Individuals make up communities which make up nations which make up the world. The source of progress therefore lies in individual will and individual action. Moreover, the advances in technology and the shift in society's thinking both point in one direction: individual empowerment. I am not promoting selfishness but self-fulfilment within the bounds of decent, moral values. Let's break down all our problems – schooling, housing, job creation – to community level. Something tangible. Something we can handle. Not an abstract national initiative where the size of the issue paralyses the mind. It's the "poor young billions" next door to you that need your help. Remember, Gross National Product is merely the sum of all the community products. Whether it's community policing, community health, community schools – these functions can be very effectively handled at community level because accountability can be rigorously enforced. "Small is beautiful" when it comes to generating very high rates of economic growth in deprived areas. Focus on the community: that's the essence of the "High Road".

I was recently having breakfast in the guest lodge at one of Anglo's gold mines. A young lady came and sat at my table. I asked her what she did. She said: "I'm a doctor here. I look after the children of employees." Then she asked me what I did. I said: "I'm chairman of this gold mine." She immediately responded: "I didn't ask you what you are, I asked what do you do." This rejoinder poleaxed me. I mean, she healed kids, she saved lives – what did I do to compare? It made me realise that we all suffer occasionally from the affliction of hiding behind our badge of office. As an antidote, therefore, when we wake up every morning, we should ask ourselves what value are we going to add to the world around us today. How are we going to make the "High Road" a reality? What are we going to *do*?

### Step by Step

They say that every long journey starts with a small step. Life is a step by step approach: incremental, not one great leap forward. Nevertheless, if we take the "High Road" we may look back on our tracks in 20 years' time and wonder at how far we have come. Moreover, the "High Road" has no final terminus called Utopia. It is a constant, never-ending search for the truth. It is the route to travel, not the place to rest.

On the way, we were always going to encounter the rapids in the stream of change. Every society in transition does some white-water-rafting. But the crew will survive, even if the raft occasionally overturns and you have to cling to it for dear life! One day, we shall enjoy the more tranquil waters downstream. The Chinese curse says "may you live in interesting times". On the contrary, there is no joy without challenge. Everyone living here at the moment may in retrospect feel privileged that they were at the turning-point in history.

186

I hope I have entertained you with this book, but most of all I hope I have lit a fire in your soul to do something about it: to make a positive difference to your community and thereby to your country and ultimately to the world at large. Hope springs eternal as long as it is accompanied by effort. No amount of darkness can put out the smallest flame. In the end, though, it's your move. Nobody can make it for you.